NEW DIRECTIONS FOR COMMUNITY COLLEGES

Arthur M. Cohen
EDITOR-IN-CHIEF

Florence B. Brawer
ASSOCIATE EDITOR

Paula Zeszotarski
PUBLICATION COORDINATOR

Dimensions of Managing Academic Affairs in the Community College

Douglas Robillard, Jr.
Philander Smith College, Little Rock, Arkansas

EDITOR

Number 109, Spring 2000

JOSSEY-BASS PUBLISHERS
San Francisco

ERIC®

Clearinghouse for Community Colleges

DIMENSIONS OF MANAGING ACADEMIC AFFAIRS IN THE COMMUNITY COLLEGE
Douglas Robillard, Jr. (ed.)
New Directions for Community Colleges, no. 109
Volume XXVIII, number 1
Arthur M. Cohen, Editor-in-Chief
Florence B. Brawer, Associate Editor

Copyright © 2000 Jossey-Bass Inc., Publishers, 350 Sansome Street, San Francisco, CA 94104.

Jossey-Bass is a registered trademark of Jossey-Bass Inc., A Wiley Company.

No part of this publication may be reproduced, stored in a retrieval system, or transmitted in any form or by any means, electronic, mechanical, photocopying, recording, scanning, or otherwise, except as permitted under Sections 107 or 108 of the 1976 United States Copyright Act, without either the prior written permission of the Publisher or authorization through payment of the appropriate per-copy fee to the Copyright Clearance Center, 222 Rosewood Drive, Danvers, MA 01923, (978) 750-8400, fax (978) 750-4744. Requests to the Publisher for permission should be addressed to the Permissions Department, John Wiley & Sons, Inc., 605 Third Avenue, New York, NY 10158-0012, (212) 850-6011, fax (212) 850-6008, e-mail: permreq@wiley.com

New Directions for Community Colleges is indexed in Current Index to Journals in Education (ERIC).

Microfilm copies of issues and articles are available in 16mm and 35mm, as well as microfiche in 105mm, through University Microfilms Inc., 300 North Zeeb Road, Ann Arbor, Michigan 48106-1346.

ISSN 0194-3081   ISBN 0-7879-5369-5

NEW DIRECTIONS FOR COMMUNITY COLLEGES is part of The Jossey-Bass Higher and Adult Education Series and is published quarterly by Jossey-Bass Inc., Publishers, 350 Sansome Street, San Francisco, California 94104-1342, in association with the ERIC Clearinghouse for Community Colleges. Periodicals postage paid at San Francisco, California, and at additional mailing offices. POSTMASTER: Send address changes to New Directions for Community Colleges, Jossey-Bass Inc., Publishers, 350 Sansome Street, San Francisco, California 94104-1342.

SUBSCRIPTIONS cost $60.00 for individuals and $107.00 for institutions, agencies, and libraries. Prices subject to change.

THE MATERIAL in this publication is based on work sponsored wholly or in part by the Office of Educational Research and Improvement, U.S. Department of Education, under contract number ED-99-CO-0010. Its contents do not necessarily reflect the views of the Department or any other agency of the U.S. Government.

EDITORIAL CORRESPONDENCE should be sent to the Editor-in-Chief, Arthur M. Cohen, at the ERIC Clearinghouse for Community Colleges, University of California, 3051 Moore Hall, Box 951521, Los Angeles, California 90095-1521. All manuscripts receive anonymous reviews by external referees.

Cover photograph © Rene Sheret, After Image, Los Angeles, California, 1990.

www.josseybass.com

Printed in the United States of America on acid-free recycled paper containing 100 percent recovered waste paper, of which at least 20 percent is postconsumer waste.

CONTENTS

EDITOR'S NOTES

Managing academic affairs encompasses an overwhelming array of tasks. The person responsible for these duties goes by different titles at different institutions. At the institutional level, the chief academic officer (CAO) or dean of instruction carries out these duties. At some colleges, a departmental-level dean also participates in academic decision making. Throughout this volume, different titles are used interchangeably to reflect the experience of the authors.

Day-to-day duties in academic management include fielding student complaints regarding grades, scheduling, determining course offerings, and handling difficult interactions with instructors. College policy needs to be invoked and examined in relation to students' wishes. Issues pertaining to faculty certainly loom large: classes need to be taught, new instructors need to be hired, existing faculty must be evaluated, and decisions on contract renewal and nonrenewal must be made.

At the programmatic level, the CAO may have to investigate the possibility of inaugurating new curricula or revising old programs. Related to this is the ever-present issue of school finances. With few exceptions, most community college deans find themselves increasingly having to do more activities with fewer resources. This condition can entail creative budgeting in order for the dean to meet instructional obligations. The increasing demand for high-tech equipment, especially in occupational programs, can well strain an already stressed budget.

The CAO also has to contend with accountability concerns. Accrediting agencies are scrutinizing the outcomes of colleges and weighing them against the institutions' stated mission. Gone are the days when the ivory tower existed separate and inviolate from the real world. Increasingly, outside funding and accrediting agencies are empowered to examine the internal workings of programs. And the dean is usually in the thick of accountability processes: compiling data, composing reports, and shepherding visiting accountability teams around campus.

With a crushing number of tasks to perform, how can the individual responsible for academic affairs survive in this high-pressure environment? The authors in this volume of *New Directions for Community Colleges* present a variety of perspectives on how a CAO can not only survive but excel under these demanding conditions.

The volume is divided into several distinct units. The first four chapters establish the CAO or dean's role in the community college context. The first chapter provides a brief overview of the literature on "deaning" and examines the origins and the evolution of the position within the academy. The title "dean" covers a bewildering array of job duties; in one institution, a dean may function as the CAO, while in another institution, a dean may function more as a midlevel manager, with responsibility for a single programmatic area. Douglas Robillard, Jr., notes that because most deans come from academic rather than managerial backgrounds, they must cultivate the human relations and fiscal skills so necessary to the smooth operation of the institution. Chapter Two discusses the dean's role as CAO for the institution. John Stuart Erwin stresses the dean's responsibility to ensure the college's academic accountability. Chapter Three examines the CAO's relationship with faculty. Drawing on his long experience as both an academic dean and a college president, Hans A. Andrews outlines the dean's roles as faculty mentor, advocate, and disciplinarian. In Chapter Four, Hans J. Kuss describes another aspect of the dean's role: confidant to the college president.

The second group of chapters examines the day-to-day issues that arise in the management of academic affairs. In Chapter Five, George L. Findlen presents five examples of crises that arise in the daily discharge of duties. He offers practical advice on how to examine crises from different angles in order to defuse their potentially explosive legal consequences. In Chapter Six, Rose Ann Findlen examines the issue of conflict among members of the college community. She suggests that conflict, far from being something to be avoided, presents an opportunity to effect constructive change within the institution. Both chapters present practical advice that can assist deans in surviving in the stressful daily environment of the college.

The next two chapters discuss aspects of budgetary and data management. In Chapter Seven, Susan A. McBride provides a useful introduction to the subject of resource management along with a beginner's glossary of budgetary terms. In Chapter Eight, George Johnston and Sharon A. R. Kristovich examine the role that the information processing staff can play in assisting the dean. They present a unique solution to the problem of information overload, defining the difference between information and data and showing how the latter can provide useful insights into the condition of the community college.

The final two chapters examine issues of professional development for deans. From her perspective in the Office of Community College Research and Leadership, Debra D. Bragg presents her views on the academic preparation for college deans. Finally, in Chapter 10, George L. Findlen describes the useful reference volumes that ought to be on every CAO's bookshelf. Rather than focusing on theory, Findlen presents a survival guide for CAOs; practical skills, not theoretical knowledge, are the emphasis in his selection of indispensable works. Geared to meet the most common contingencies, the references presented in this chapter provide a fitting coda to the volume's theme of managing academic affairs in the community college.

Douglas Robillard, Jr.
Editor

DOUGLAS ROBILLARD, JR., is interim vice president for academic affairs at Philander Smith College in Little Rock, Arkansas. Previously he served as a curriculum specialist and Title III activity director at the district office of Illinois Eastern Community Colleges.

1

This chapter discusses the multitude of tasks that community college academic deans perform and the evolution of the role of dean through the present. It also examines current job descriptions and discusses some of the skills that are essential to the dean's survival.

Toward a Definition of Deaning

Douglas Robillard, Jr.

The first obstacle to performing research on deans is the lack of definition associated with the term *dean*. Vaughan (1990) reports that in 1966, a newly inaugurated community college president asked him if he would like to serve as dean of instruction. "What is a dean of instruction?" asked Vaughan. In response, the president told Vaughan, "I'll be damned if I know, but if you want the position, we'll find out together" (p. ix). Vaughan's anecdote is telling because it reveals the ambiguous nature of the deanship. In another volume, Vaughan (1989) offers this definition: "Dean of instruction is the most commonly-used title given to the person who is responsible for the instructional program at community colleges" (p. 109). Despite Vaughan's definition, we will see that the position often entails responsibility for more than instructional programs. It may be that the ambiguity associated with the position of dean exists because the position is still evolving.

Until recently, a review of the literature on "deaning" would turn up surprisingly slim pickings. One authority observes that university presidents and professors have been exhaustively studied but that "'middle management,' the deanship, represents a void in our database" (Dill, 1980, p. 92). The volume of literature has increased somewhat since 1980, according to Creswell and England (1994). Although academic chairs have been a recently popular research topic, "the position of dean has received little scholarly attention" (Creswell and England, 1994, p. 7). In fact, between Dill and Creswell and England, only three book-length studies on the deanship were published: Morris (1981), Tucker and Bryan (1988), and Vaughan (1990). Of the three, only Vaughan specifically addresses the community college deanship in *Pathway to the Presidency*. More recently, Martin and Samuels's *First Among Equals* (1997) has added to the literature, but the field still seems under researched.

This problem of the dean's multitudinous duties is particularly acute at the community college level. Vaughan (1990) recounts the story of a community college dean of instruction who was instructed to contact his counterparts at eight senior-level institutions. The dean's problem? He determined that he needed to contact thirty-eight different individuals at the eight institutions in order to reach all of his counterparts. The scope of this individual's duties at the community college was actually greater than that of his counterparts at the universities. Vaughan's (1990) summary provides insight into the duties of the dean of instruction at a community college: "Deans of instruction at community colleges perform most of the duties assigned to the chief academic officer at small, four-year private colleges, . . . many of the duties performed by provosts or academic vice presidents at major universities, . . . many of the duties performed by the deans of the various schools or colleges within major universities" (p. 110).

In the community college, the dean is responsible for a greater variety, if not a greater volume, of activities than this person's counterparts at four-year institutions. This condition results partly from a shortage of funds and personnel at community colleges. It is also indicative of the evolving nature of the deanship. As we will see, deans came into the American higher education scene relatively late. Consequently, the position is still evolving.

Origin of the Species

Gould (1964) offers evidence that the deanship emerged in the late nineteenth century, "when presidents began to feel the need for someone to relieve them of record- and housekeeping chores" (p. 6). Early on, the dean functioned as an administrative assistant for the president. The nature of these housekeeping duties has changed over time. As far back as 1930, Dean Herbert E. Hawkes of Columbia College could remark, "There is no such thing as a standardized dean. There is a dean of this and that college, but I have never seen any two deans who could exchange places and retain the same duties" (Gould, 1964, p. 9). In tracing the evolution of the deanship between Hawkes's time and his own, thirty years later, Gould notes a progression in the roles of the dean "from almost sole concern with students, through a phase when students and curriculum were his largest responsibilities, to a period when curriculum and faculty demanded the greatest part of his energies, and finally to a place where his major concern is the faculty alone" (p. 10). The progression Gould traces is a shift of emphasis away from the students toward the faculty. The "dean of men," "dean of women," and "dean of the college" roles have given way to a greater focus on faculty.

At the community college, the key dean, the dean of instruction, works closely with the faculty in managing the college's academic programs. A glance at recent job opening announcements for community college deans of instruction shows us the state of the position now, thirty-five years after Gould. The current job responsibilities for deans illustrate how the position's duties have developed since Gould's time. The *Chronicle of Higher Education*, September 10, 1999, contains several advertisements for dean-level positions. Applicants for a dean of arts and sciences position at Southeastern Community College in Iowa must be willing to assume leadership responsibility for faculty, curriculum planning and development, staffing, evaluation, and budgetary administration. In the same issue, Cochise College in Arizona seeks candidates who can assess programs, foster partnerships among internal and external constituents, and manage conflict. These lists of duties illustrate the qualifications deemed necessary for the dean in today's community college. Not incidentally, they comprise a short list of the qualifications necessary to help a dean survive in the pressure-filled community college environment. Experience in administration and supervision is obviously quite important: the dean must hire and evaluate faculty. Experience with budgetary matters will help the dean to negotiate the fiscal needs of the college.

The prospective dean must also have experience in program assessment. In addition, the dean must exercise a host of interpersonal and supervisory skills in developing partnerships with outside entities. Further, the responsibility for faculty development requires skill and tact in human relations. The prospective dean will also be engaged in accountability issues, as evidenced by the program evaluation and review components.

Productivity and Accountability

The growing importance of outside accrediting bodies and the need for institutional accountability is another important factor in the development of the dean's position at the beginning of the century. It is now a given that the community college dean must focus on the quality and productivity of academic programs.

In one example of this effort to hold postsecondary institutions to greater fiscal and programmatic accountability, the Illinois Community College Board and Illinois Board of Higher Education developed the combined *Priorities/Quality/Productivity* (PQP) Program Review. This state-mandated annual report focuses not only on certain vocational and technical programs and requires colleges to evaluate them, but also specifies that overall academic, administrative, and public service productivity must be taken into account as well. Instructional programs are evaluated from the standpoint of unit cost, enrollment, and job outlooks for graduates, all considerations that come under the purview of deans. A program can be found satisfactory, in need of revision, or in need of termination. The PQP report also includes a spreadsheet, intended to illustrate how funds from revised or discontinued programs are to be reallocated. In addition, each year's PQP report includes "Special Focus Questions," pinpointing areas for institutional research. In order to grapple with the challenges presented by this particular measure of accountability, the dean will certainly have to deal with issues of cost-effectiveness, needs analysis, and staffing. However, PQP is simply one measure of accountability; other outside entities such as regional and discipline-specific accrediting groups also vie for the dean's attention.

Human Relations Skills

In his pioneering study *Deaning* (1981) Morris states, "Upward of four-fifths of the cost of running an academic establishment consists of wages and salaries of employees. . . . The dean's primary task, therefore, is to purchase and deploy what budget makers call personal 'services' and the time, energy, and special skills they represent" (p. 102). Cohen and Brawer (1996) concur with Morris when they ask, "Where does the money go? Half is devoted to instruction; 22 percent to administration; 10 percent to student services; 11 percent to physical plant operation and maintenance; and around 2.5 percent each to libraries, public service, and scholarships" (pp. 151–152). These figures are instructive for prospective deans since they indicate how a community college divides its expenditures. The 50 percent figure for instruction deals with people, not equipment. Even with innovations like the Internet and distance learning, education continues to be a labor-intensive occupation.

In response to Vaughan's (1990) queries about the skills requirements for deanships, a group of deans responded, "People skills" (p. 17). Certainly in mediating among students, faculty, administration, and the president, the dean must exercise good cooperation, troubleshooting, and listening skills. The dean's survival depends partly on the ability to work constructively with diverse constituencies, some of whom may be at odds with one another or in competition for scarce resources.

With such demands for time and effort placed on deans, perhaps they may be inclined to let slide apparently less pressing concerns such as the budget. As one of Vaughan's (1990) interviewees points out, there are gaps in the dean's vocational preparation: "The void—and I think it's probably common in a lot of deans—is that we tend to come from academic backgrounds. We don't come from backgrounds that emphasize leadership and management" (p. 47).

Budgetary Skills

Although people skills head the list, another important attribute is skill in working with a budget (Vaughan, 1990). Leaders of academic programs are often more interested in the content of their programs than in the fiscal considerations that make these programs possible in the first place. All components of the academic program are fueled by the budget: salaries, benefits, classroom space, supplies, and instructional equipment. This brings to the fore the issue of financial management.

Perhaps the clearest indication of the fundamental importance of good financial know-how on the part of the academic dean is found in the opening chapter of Tucker and Bryan's *The Academic Dean*. Entitled "The Perfect Dean," this chapter is a deliberate exercise in wishful thinking. It poses the question, "What would the perfect life be like for the academic dean?" (p. 1). Virtually every point of this perfectly fulfilled life touches on financial security. The dean's budget would be not merely adequate; "it would be generous" (Tucker and Bryan, 1988, p. 1). With high faculty salaries, overflowing instructional equipment dollars, living wages for graduate assistants, and plenty of money for research and honoraria, cash flow would not be a problem. Such is the Edenic fantasy of the perfect dean. Of course, the term *utopia* is derived from Greek roots that mean "nowhere"; utopian societies, even in academe, truly exist nowhere! However, the garden is barred to us; deans, like everyone else since Eden, must make their living through the sweat of their brows.

In the world as it is, deans must guarantee that the college's students are properly educated, and "if this task must be accomplished with an inadequate budget, a faculty burdened with all the imperfections of mortality, and an administration that is neither benevolent nor omniscient, the dean must learn the art of management" (Tucker and Bryan, 1988, p. 3). Without funds to support them, activities and academic programs languish. It is clear that apart from exceptional human relation skills, the dean must also be able to make intelligent use of resources, which entails working with and within a budget.

Hankin (1996) concurs with Vaughan's interviewee on the problem of lack of vocational preparation among new administrators: "Administrators often complain about their lack of training in fiscal matters and their limited capacity to respond to critics who claim that 'philosophy follows finances,' or that resources are devoted to frivolous courses. . . . Administrators need to tackle this problem with the understanding that budgets are educational programs written out in dollar figures" (p. 43).

Hankin's point is well taken and dovetails neatly with Vandament (1989) and Vaughan (1990). Deans generally come from an academic rather than a managerial background. They have extensive schooling, teaching experience, and familiarity with the landscape of higher education, but their academic and work experience often has not prepared them for dealing with fiscal matters. The paradigm shift that Hankin (1996) suggests is that deans need to see the budget as not only an outward expression of the institution's mission, but as the embodiment of the institution's academic programs in quantifiable, monetary terms.

Tucker and Bryan (1988) offer a cogent outline of the factors that prudent deans should consider as they establish budget priorities:

a. The strengths and weaknesses of the programs in the college
b. The internal arrangements of the college with other colleges, schools, or units in the institution
c. The needs of society
d. The opportunities for the students of the institution
e. The desires and aspirations of the faculty [p. 6]

Tucker and Bryan are quick to point out that there are no easy rules for establishing budgetary priorities or for weighing considerations against one another. Each case must be taken separately, considered on its own merits. Considerations vary depending on the institution and its own history.

In dealing with human and material capital, it is important to inaugurate long-range planning. Cohen and Brawer (1996) ask, "What measures of institutional productivity can be introduced so that increased costs can be justified?" (p. 159). Vandament (1989) offers some advice for institutional research in a comprehensive "checklist of unit-specific issues" to be examined at appropriate times in the budget cycle. The checklist includes audits of instructional equipment, staffing requirements to meet program commitments, and alternative sources of funding.

Conclusion

It is clear from the research that the position of dean at a community college is a challenging job. Deans must mediate among students, faculty, administration, and staff. They must be careful stewards of resources and offer guidance in how funds should be allocated and reallocated. Finally, they must cope with both internal program evaluation and external accountability mandates.

References

Cohen, A. M., and Brawer, F. B. *The American Community College.* San Francisco: Jossey-Bass, 1996.

Creswell, J. W., and England, M. E. "Improving Informational Resources for Academic Deans and Chairpersons." In M. K. Kinnick (ed.), *Providing Useful Information for Deans and Department Chairs.* San Francisco: Jossey-Bass, 1994.

Dill, W. R. "The Deanship: An Unstable Craft." In D. E. Griffiths and D. J. McCarty (eds.), *The Dilemma of the Deanship.* Danville, Ill.: Interstate, 1980.

Gould, J. W. *The Academic Deanship.* New York: Teachers College Press, 1964.

Hankin, J. N. "The Door That Never Closes: Continuing Education Needs of Community College Leaders." In J. C. Palmer and S. G. Katsinas (eds.), *Graduate and Continuing Education for Community College Leaders: What It Means Today.* San Francisco: Jossey-Bass, 1996.

Martin, J., Samels, J. E., and others. *First Among Equals.* Baltimore: Johns Hopkins University Press, 1997.

Morris, V. C. *Deaning.* Urbana: University of Illinois Press, 1981.

Tucker, A., and Bryan, R. A. *The Academic Dean.* New York: Macmillan, 1988.

Vandament, W. E. *Managing Money in Higher Education.* San Francisco: Jossey-Bass, 1989.

Vaughan, G. B. *Leadership in Transition.* Washington, D.C.: Community College Press, 1989.

Vaughan, G. B. *Pathway to the Presidency.* Washington, D.C.: Community College Press, 1990.

DOUGLAS ROBILLARD, JR., is interim vice president for academic affairs at Philander Smith College in Little Rock, Arkansas. Previously he served as a curriculum specialist and Title III activity director at the district office of Illinois Eastern Community Colleges.

2

*This chapter examines the role of the dean as chief aca-
demic officer with primary responsibility for curriculum
development and the instructional integrity of the college.*

The Dean as Chief Academic Officer

John Stuart Erwin

The chief academic officer (CAO) at a college is the person primarily
responsible for its instructional integrity and curriculum development. Each
college needs a single individual who has primary accountability for instruction. In this new millennium, colleges face not only constant change but
also the challenge of the increased speed of change. An explosion of
advances makes it incumbent on the CAO to be informed, flexible, and
technologically knowledgeable in the emerging academic world.

Role of the Chief Academic Officer

Roles for the CAO of a college used to be defined in terms of organizational
structure (Brown, 1984). The CAO reported up to a chief executive officer
and the governing board; down to the deans, chairs, and others who
reported to the CAO; sideways to colleagues in student, administrative,
development, and financial services; and obliquely to those with titles like
assistant dean, assistant vice president, and associate dean. Finally, the
CAO had to have a campus, systemwide, and national perspective on the
college.

An administrator who has worked up to the position of CAO of a college is already familiar with, and probably very successful at appreciating
the importance of, these multiple perspectives. As an alternative to the pyra-
mid relations, Kotter (1999) illustrates the importance of leadership in
choosing strategies for change, dependency, and networks. His approach to
management accentuates the need for a variety of methods. Face-to-face
contact with employees, influence and persuasion, and indirect methods are
all arrows in the quiver of an effective leader. Kotter refers to the ability to
use a variety of methods as "investing power."

Today's CAO must have a firm grasp of processes, especially how to initiate a process of change. Various models exist for change. Two fundamental ones are bureaucratic and participatory (Brown, 1984). The bureaucratic model is characterized by centralized decision making, little delegated responsibility, formality, budget control, and clear organizational divisions. The bureaucratic model has validity during times of extreme crisis, such as when student enrollments decline or there exist financial exigencies. The weakness of this model is that it hinders creativity and implementation of change. Employees are stifled, and distrust and low morale are reflected in the college climate. A bureaucratic leader can control the institution, but the motivation of faculty, staff, and other administrators is thwarted. Minimal cooperation and creativity blocks the successful development and implementation of change.

Participatory leadership is characterized by an open campus, shared vision, and the value that people are the most important part of the institution. Leaders are motivated to listen to employee ideas, they encourage open information and faculty and staff development, and they exude trust and confidence. Problem solving, not fear and blame, is the focus of participatory management. The CAO who uses a participatory model decentralizes daily activities and empowers each employee to be a decision maker.

One of the best descriptions for realizing participatory management is explained by Blanchard, Carlos, and Randolph (1999) as the "challenge of moving to empowerment." They present three keys to accomplishing empowered employees: information sharing, awareness of boundaries for responsibility and autonomy, and development teams to replace the hierarchy in the institution.

Colleges and CAOs may choose to implement various aspects of the Total Quality Management movement. Colleges are moving from "hierarchical, function-based structures to horizontal, integrated workplaces organized around empowered individuals and self-directed work teams as the means to achieve sustainable process changes" (Graham and LeBaron, 1994, p. xv). The CAO has a vested interest in the successful implementation of this team approach for faculty, staff, and administration. The results may be sustainable for longer periods of time and consequently relieve the CAO of the difficulty of constant cross-institutional communication.

Covey (1990) describes six conditions of empowerment:

Win-win agreement, a psychological contract between a manager and someone supervised. The manager and the employee agree on expectations regarding desired results, guidelines, resources, accountabilities and consequences. The goal is to support the individual's self-direction and self-control so that within the guidelines, desired results are accomplished.
Self-supervision, which is realized in the progression within the win-win agreement.
Helpful structures and systems, which evolve from personal and organizational consequences.

Self-evaluation, which creates accountability.

Character, which contains at least three attributes: integrity (habits, values, deeds), maturity (courage balanced with consideration), and abundance mentality (positively harnessing resources).

Skills for empowering others, which include communication, planning, and synergistic problem solving.

The Covey model offers the CAO an opportunity to strengthen a college's instructional enterprise by establishing these six conditions for empowerment and receiving the rewards that come from the individual faculty, colleagues, and staff who become self-supervised and empowered. One of the most important aspects of this model is the emphasis placed on problem solving. Many CAOs face a constant barrage of crises from the time of arrival in the morning until the day's work is done. Indeed, work for the CAO can be defined in terms of problem solving or conflict resolution. But much of this problem-solving aspect of the job may be changed if empowerment is practiced. In the early stages of empowerment, teams may be allowed to make decisions that are less complex. Keighley suggests that decisions like maintaining housekeeping and safety, internal customer contact, and measuring quality may be made in the initial stages of empowerment. At the second stage of change, decisions like determining training needs, production scheduling and control, and managing suppliers may be made (Blanchard, Carlos, and Randolph, 1999). At a college, the CAO may wish to empower assistant deans, chairs, and faculty in order to lessen the onslaught of crisis decision making. For example, a team may be formed that deals only with student concerns, another that handles textbook selection, and one that resolves student academic appeals.

When those who are supervised by the CAO are empowered to resolve conflicts and make decisions, then the CAO spends less time on problem solving and more time on management. Empowered individuals also increase college morale. A CAO can positively contribute to that healthy climate by practicing the Covey model or a modification that accents resolutions and decisions at the most basic levels of the organization.

Absolute democracy does not work well in an academic institution (Covey, 1990). A successful participatory leader will have to decide which activities need centralized control and which ones do not need direct oversight. One of Covey's guiding principles is to keep leadership training, development of mission and goals, and evaluation processes centralized, while decentralizing daily activities.

Other Factors That Affect the CAO

CAOs function within each of these two models and many variations in between. There is a great variance in the ability and willingness of presidents to delegate authority. A CAO is more likely to experience broader delegation when enrollments are increasing and the budget is balanced. During times of instability, a president is likely to maintain tighter control over the major college operations (Dill, 1980; Brown, 1984). CAOs at two-year technical and community colleges not only experience variations in management systems and styles, but also know about potential tumultuous changes in budget and enrollments, especially if they have worked under more than one president.

At least two authors have written about the changes that are unique to community colleges, the differences in each college's demographics, and the effects on the role of the dean as an academic officer (Powell, 1983; Beaver, 1993). Beaver found that deans who have retained their position for five to nine years in colleges with enrollments of fewer than twenty-five hundred students are less satisfied with daily activities than are deans from larger schools. This was partly the result of the larger salary and more benefits accorded the deans of larger institutions (Beaver, 1993).

However, the greatest attention of deans in community and technical colleges was devoted to instruction, not money and financial solvency (Powell, 1983). The size of the college was not a factor in determining the centrality of instruction. As the primary educational leader of the campus, the CAO has a legal obligation for maintaining and developing the integrity of academic programs and determining whether they meet the proper state, division, and departmental approvals. Sometimes the maze of paper, people, and politics creates a barrier to assessing a program.

Curriculum Development and the CAO

A primary task of the CAO is to ensure that the college has properly conducted its curriculum development with respect to internal and state regulations. This is a daunting task when a college catalogue is revised every year or two. As technologies and subject areas advance, the need for curriculum changes is paramount. The CAO needs to apply the regulations and inform the curriculum approval process in such a manner as to encourage course improvements while maintaining the college checkpoints in the approval process. Cross-departmental and divisional curricula offer the greatest challenge to the CAO because they require clear and frequent communication between and among the faculty and chairs (Baker, 1999).

Each state has its own version of a regulatory agency. In Illinois, for example, it is the Illinois Community College Board; in Ohio, the Ohio Board of Regents; and in Iowa, the Iowa Department of Education. These agencies assign certain parameters around the degree requirements, including the course, contact, and lab hours, as well as the feasibility measures for a new program or course. These measures include, but are not restricted to, the local demand for the content or program, disallowing redundancy, financial support, and the ability, where possible, for university transfer. As one researcher noted, there is a "delicate and complicated boundary where the life of the community college meets the life of state government" (Cohen and others, 1994, p. 101).

Striving for balance in the curriculum requires the CAO to support and implement existing processes for changing the curriculum. At San Jose City College in California, staff and faculty were asked to participate in a curriculum planning process with the following steps (Brobst and Kanton, 1992):

1. Analyzing the strengths and weaknesses of the curriculum in terms of the mission for community colleges
2. Identifying fiscal parameters which affect the balance of offerings
3. Recommending ways in which courses required for the major can be offered with regularity, on a consistent schedule, and within fiscal constraints
4. Determining the appropriate percentages of the courses required for the A.A. or A.S. degree, the certificate only, entry-level versus majors, general education, and so forth
5. Recommending an appropriate configuration of course offerings to ensure a balanced curriculum that assigns priorities within disciplines and divisions and with attention to future programs

After these steps, a balanced curriculum, based on the expertise of the various college constituencies, was developed to meet students' educational goals (Cohen and others, 1994).

The CAO and the Community

An integral part of the community college mission is community service. High expectations in the community result from the success of the community college in extending educational services.

The CAO has ultimate responsibility for the breadth and quality of what the college offers to the community. Although many colleges have a dean or director over community and adult education, this position often reports to the CAO. Edmund J. Gleazer, Jr., a former president of the American Association of Community and Junior Colleges, frequently argued for the college to be the center of community life (Cohen, 1992). Gleazer believed the college was "the nexus of all community educative activities, to be the agency that uplifts its community directly by intervening in every aspect of community life, to reach out beyond the campus and touch the citizenry with an array of forums, fairs, and resource centers accessible to everyone" (Cohen, 1992, p. 177). No community college has fully realized Gleazer's lofty goal, but the quest to attain, even partially, the intermingling of community life and the college's mission has left an indelible imprint on the community college movement's history.

Each CAO will benefit from a mechanism to measure the community's educational needs. Surveys are essential, but the direct contact through existing programs and services is an invaluable avenue for communication. Craft fairs, cultural extravaganzas, job fairs, workforce development, business and industry training, continuing education units, certification, licensure, and hobbies become the venues by which community engagement occurs for the community college. Residual benefits abound for the CAO who supports a comprehensive community service program. College foundations may receive more dollars. Marketing for the college receives a boost by the positive word-of-mouth recommendations from satisfied students. Employers reap the harvest of higher-qualified employees and applicants.

The CAO and Learning Communities

Recently Terry O'Banion (1997) issued a challenge to community colleges to embrace the concept of becoming learning communities: "Many colleges are involved in the process of transforming their cultures: marketing to new groups of students, developing assessment and outcomes measures, building creative linkages to their communities, applying new technologies to improve teaching and management, increasing standards for students and teachers, flattening organizational structures, decentralizing decision making, building alliances with business and industry, applying Continuous Quality Improvement and Total Quality Management processes. . . . But in many cases these actions have been the usual extensions and add-ons leading only to modest change in the status quo. In most cases, what students learn and how students learn have remained relatively unchanged" (p. xvi).

For a CAO to institute effective change that assists in building a learning community at a college, two imperatives are evident: the student comes first and more learning for more students at a lower cost. Senge (1990) defines a learning organization as one in which all employees are involved as continuous learners to improve the practices and programs developed to achieve the purposes of the organization. To accomplish this environmental change, collaboration emerges as the key value in overcoming the old structures. Two research experts on building learning communities underscore the importance of shared resources by claiming that the most successful colleges have a system that "achieves efficiency through partnerships" (Harlacher and Gollattscheck, 1996).

At the Maricopa Community Colleges in Phoenix, Arizona, a massive effort has developed to realize the goal of a learning community. Several lessons can be drawn from the experience. One is that collaboration processes proved the most useful for generating support for change. Another is that the CEO had to endorse and support the vision of a learner-centered institution (O'Banion, 1997). By practicing collaboration, lending moral support for the changes, and constantly reinforcing that changes take time, effort, and constancy, the CAO exemplifies the precepts of a learning community. Another lesson that Maricopa learned was the importance of involving students, faculty, internal resources, and external consultants in change processes (O'Banion, 1997).

The CAO plays a pivotal role in implementing the changes needed for a learning community (Freed, Klugman, and Fife, 1997). It may be that assessment of student learning needs faculty classroom involvement. The CAO can create workshops on classroom assessment or garner college funds to pay for the assessment instruments if they are externally scored. Also, by creating or supporting the professional development of faculty, staff, and academic administrators through the linkages drawn from performance appraisals and evaluations to an individual growth plan, the CAO energizes the entire learning community. The coordination of multiple constituencies lands squarely in the CAO's lap of responsibility. Because the CAO transcends divisions, departments, and areas, he or she can broker the changes needed for creating a learning community by applying collaboration in practice and adhering to participatory management as a philosophy.

Instructional Technology and the CAO

The technology and information age demands that the CAO be cognizant of the opportunities for the college during times of rapid advancements. College developments in instructional technology are expensive. James R. Coffman (Martin, Samels, and others, 1997) describes the CAO's activity in this regard as leveraging, that is, directing the time, talent, and resources of the college toward instructional technology. Demographics point us toward an essential change in instructional delivery from traditional place- and time-bound courses to open entry, exit, and individualized methods.

Coffman outlines several emerging trends that impinge on instructional development. The number of high school graduates will increase by a projected 20 percent shortly after 2000. Future students will be much more computer literate and oriented toward television and interactive technology. Taxpayers and tuition payers have become cynical about a perceived lack of attention to teaching. The typical curriculum has become too long and inflexible. The information explosion is a reality and will continue to affect the needs of students.

Two ingredients are critically important to the CAO's successful support of instructional technology. Foremost in a faculty union environment is contractual support for the development and delivery of electronically purveyed instructional materials. Belleville Area Community College, in Belleville, Illinois, and Cincinnati State Technical and Community College, Cincinnati, Ohio, have faculty contracts that outline support for the development and delivery of instructional technology. The compensation for the development of distance courses (such as telecourses, web based, Internet, and intranet) and the actual teaching of those courses needs to be included in the contract language. One of the most sensitive areas for contract discussion for electronically purveyed instructional materials is copyright. Who owns the materials, for how long, and under what conditions? Legal advice can assist in reaching a mutually acceptable outcome.

The second ingredient for a CAO's successful support of instructional technology is to have some mechanism for training. Some colleges have created instructional design centers, while other colleges have periodic workshops. Technical expertise and sensitivity to instructional issues for creating distance courses are factors that need consideration.

Although the CAO does not need to know the details of instructional technology, it is important for him or her to select faculty and academic administrators who have some combination of technical ability and human relation skills to ensure the ongoing success of educational technology on the campus. A key person is the chief information officer, who may work with the CAO in order to set priorities in classroom advancements and obtaining and maintaining the computer and electronic infrastructure for excellent technical instruction.

Besides leveraging resources, developing contractual language, training faculty, and working with the chief information officer to set priorities for instructional technology, the CAO must be committed to cultivating an interest in teaching technology among the faculty. Even in a small college, a few faculty will emerge who have an interest in innovations for their classroom. To steer them toward technology and encourage these professional pioneers will lay a firm foundation to support future expansion. The success of the CAO and instructional technology depends on the commitment and skills of the college's faculty.

Conclusion

The instructional significance of the college revolves around the chief academic officer. Whether as a dean or academic vice president, the CAO has primary responsibility for coordinating curriculum development and maintaining the college's instructional integrity. The role of the CAO has been expanding as new management styles, curriculum creation, community engagement, emphasis on learning communities, and developments in instructional technology influence the activities associated with the job.

References

Baker, G. A. *A Handbook on the Community College in America.* Westport, Conn.: Greenwood Press, 1999.

Beaver, M. O. *A Profile of Engineering Technology Deans: Characteristics and Functions of Engineering Technology Deans on Two-Year Campuses.* Athens: Ohio University, 1993.

Blanchard, K., Carlos, J. P., and Randolph, A. *The 3 Keys to Empowerment.* San Francisco: Berrett-Koehler, 1999.

Brobst, D., and Kanton, M. J. *Change to the Instructional Policies/Curriculum Committee's Subcommittees on Curriculum Balance.* San Jose, Calif.: San Jose City College, 1992.

Brown, D. G. (ed.). *The Chief Academic Officer: Argus on Campus.* New Directions in Higher Education, no. 47. San Francisco: Jossey-Bass, 1984.

Cohen, A. M., ed., *Perspectives on the Community College: Essays by John Lomlardi.* Washington, D.C.: ERIC Clearinghouse on Community Colleges, American Association of Community Colleges and American Council on Education, 1992.

Cohen, A. M., and others. *Managing Community Colleges.* San Francisco: Jossey-Bass, 1994.

Covey, S. R. *Principle Centered Leadership.* New York: Simon & Schuster, 1990.

Dill, W. R. *The Dilemma of the Deanship.* Danville, Ill.: Interstate, 1980.

Freed, J., Klugman, M. B., and Fife, J. D. *A Culture for Academic Excellence.* Washington, D.C.: ASHE-ERIC, George Washington University, 1997.

Graham, M. A., and LeBaron, M. J. *The Horizontal Solution.* San Francisco: Jossey-Bass, 1994.

Harlacher, E. L., and Gollattscheck, J. F. *The Community Building College: Leading the Way to Community Revitalization.* Washington, D.C.: Community College Press, 1996.

Kotter, J. P. *What Leaders Really Do.* Cambridge, Mass.: President and Harvard Fellows, 1999.

Martin, J., Samels, J. E., and others. *First Among Equals.* Baltimore: Johns Hopkins University Press, 1997.

O'Banion, T. *A Learning College for the 21st Century.* Phoenix, Arizona: American Council of Education and Oryx Press, 1997.

Powell, T. A. *A Descriptive Investigation of the Status of Deans of Instruction in Community Colleges and Technical Colleges.* Columbus: Ohio State University, 1983.

Senge, P. *The Fifth Discipline.* New York: Doubleday, 1990.

JOHN STUART ERWIN is the academic vice president of Cincinnati State Technical and Community College, Cincinnati, Ohio.

3

The academic dean carries a major responsibility for the teaching and learning outcomes of a community college. Assisting faculty to obtain a high level of teaching competence is paramount to the role.

The Dean and the Faculty

Hans A. Andrews

There may be no greater administrative role within community colleges than that of dean (or vice president) of instruction. It is a role that demands highly competent people with a good sense of fairness, a broad view of teaching and learning, and an ability to put together personnel, curriculum, and budget issues. This chapter looks at the key factors for the dean of instruction in moving to develop a high-quality teaching faculty and achieve strong student learning outcomes.

A Pressure Role

The dean's role is a pressure role. Changes in curriculum, negotiations for salaries and working conditions for faculty, issues of excellence in the classroom, and finding funding to support the needs and efforts of the faculty create a pressure-cooker atmosphere of issues and needs within the institution. The dean becomes the person who blends these issues and needs in order to make outstanding teaching and learning the outcome of the institution.

The pressure builds as the dean must determine organizational priorities. In my role as a dean, I was often asked, "How do you find time to do faculty evaluation?" Consistently, my response was, "It is one of my top priorities." The pressure comes when curriculum needs, advisory committee meetings, state department changes, budget development, catalogue and schedules with tight deadlines, state and local grant development support, board meetings, and other committee meetings on campus must all be included with many other responsibilities.

The college dean needs the respect of the faculty. The dean needs to be able to identify with the faculty through previous teaching experiences. Excellence in classroom teaching is undoubtedly the most important prerequisite for a person in this position. Other traits that are essential in this role are honesty, integrity, a "can-do" attitude, fairness, consistency, and the ability to negotiate and to solve problems.

Faculty Turnover

In a North Central Association accrediting self-study several years ago, I noted that a 50 percent turnover of faculty would be expected in the coming decade. When the college president read that figure, he called me into his office to have me defend this percentage. A close review of the previous nine years had showed the college already had a 47 percent turnover of faculty. We ended up agreeing on the 50 percent.

The dean and division or department heads on campus can usually identify fairly accurately which faculty will most likely leave the institution within one to five years. Some faculty leave as they retire. Others may leave due to deficiencies identified in their performance through the faculty evaluation process. The attrition of those who pursue better economic opportunities is harder to predict.

Replacing faculty is easier in some academic fields of study than in others. As the twenty-first century begins, there are no identifiable problems attracting faculty in English and social science. It is much more difficult to find and attract qualified electronics or nursing instructors. Nursing faculty, for example, seldom come to colleges prepared as teaching faculty. Moreover, community businesses and medical facilities offer both groups options and pay that two-year colleges seldom can meet. Some nursing positions, for example, command a salary that is 50 to 60 percent higher than colleges can pay. In 1998 I conducted an eighteen-campus survey of two-year colleges in Illinois. Not one of the eighteen colleges had a single application on file for nursing faculty to draw on for the future or for any last-minute faculty replacements.

One task that is currently challenging college deans is meeting the needs of the expanding Asian and Mexican populations in the West, Southwest, and Southeast United States. In addition, finding a diverse faculty will continue to stretch the imagination of those responsible for hiring at the colleges.

Marzano and Andrews (1990–1991) suggested a "growing-your-own" approach to developing future faculty for two-year colleges. Identification of potential teachers from the student body would be followed up with a financial commitment to assist such students in their last two years of a baccalaureate and possibly even through a master's degree. The students would then have an agreement to return for a specified number of years to teach at their home community college.

Faculty turnover will create one of the major areas of challenge for community college deans over the next ten to fifteen years. Attracting and keeping a qualified, competent, and diverse faculty to meet the emerging needs of students will be as great a task as it has ever been for these colleges.

Board Support for Teaching: Policy Development

Community college boards of trustees have the legal responsibility to develop policies and rights given to them by state statutes and legislation. In most states, they may also establish their own rules, policies, and procedures to make for smooth-running operations at the college. They also establish the legal basis for much of what happens at the college.

The college dean, along with department and division chairs and faculty, can have a significant impact on the establishment of such policies and procedures. It is important that they deal with developing excellence in the areas of instruction, evaluation of faculty and staff, awarding of tenure, recognition programs, student rights, due process, discipline and dismissal concerns.

Trustees support administrators, faculty, and staff through well-developed policies and procedures. Administrators who are challenged by students, staff, or outside people and agencies need to be in a strong legal position. If the administration and faculty follow the college procedures as approved by the board of trustees, they should feel secure that the board will be there to support them.

A board of trustees can relax a bit knowing they have policies and procedures that speak to the main concerns that arise within the college. Policies on personnel, faculty hiring, faculty evaluation, and the approval process of documents that are developed for public consumption (such as catalog, faculty handbooks, and qualifications handbooks) gain a legal strength and status when the trustees approve them. The dean and faculty can also rest better knowing that by properly administering the college policies, they will have the backing of the top administrators and the board of trustees in times of challenge.

The role of the dean may include recommending new policies or improvements to existing policies. These recommendations must have been developed with faculty and other internal support and been accepted by the college president before taking them to a board for adoption.

Evaluation and Faculty Buy-In

The dean will find no greater area of satisfaction than that of recognizing faculty who are serving students well and obtaining positive feedback from the dean and department and division chairpersons. The majority of the faculty will be evaluated favorably. A few will be troublesome and need an agreed-on development plan or some form of remediation to improve. Occasionally a faculty member will have to be considered for termination. It is important that those who are developing or revising a faculty evaluation system consult faculty and include them in the process. This is a process area in the college that needs a spirit of cooperation and a feeling of trust. If administrators who are supervising faculty members are trusted by the faculty, putting together a meaningful system of administrative in-class evaluation will be a much easier task.

The forms that evaluation usually takes are administrative, student, peer, self, or a combination of more than one of these. How much use is made of student, peer, and self-evaluation in the evaluation of faculty needs to be considered seriously. Andrews (1995) identified the many concerns that exist in these three types of evaluation processes. Administrative evaluation of faculty is the strongest in terms of being legally defensible, and it can also be most positive for faculty if carried out by administrators trusted by the faculty. The deans must earn this trust with their faculty members.

Administering and carrying out important roles in evaluation, budget development, travel support, and handling of problem areas need to be done in an objective and even-handed manner. Being an exceptional listener and carrying out promises made are necessary administrative skills. Faculty will soon let it be known if they think that the dean is biased and unfair or carrying out policies properly and improving the institutional climate for teaching and learning.

Administrative evaluation gives the dean and department heads the opportunity to assist in teaching improvement early in the teacher's work at the college. Suggestions for improvements can be specific and in writing. Individual faculty members can be encouraged or assigned to visit other faculty members' classes to observe specific teaching methods. Having a program of evaluation for more senior faculty ensures that quality in instruction will continue. Some of the outcomes of this evaluation are awarding of tenure, or continuing contracts where tenure is not awarded, and recognition for outstanding performance. Improved instruction is the main outcome for the students.

Faculty Development. Licata and Andrews (1992) found many gaps between how successful faculty evaluation and development systems were viewed by faculty leaders as compared to how they were seen by the administrators in the same colleges. This study summarized surveys from a nineteen-state area in the North Central Association accrediting district.

Administrators thought they were doing a much better job of evaluating the faculty than the faculty did in those same institutions. A major concern of a large number of the faculty leaders was that there were no outcomes of the evaluation process. Good teachers went unnoticed and were not given development plans, while poor teachers were given no improvement plans or sanctions to work on for improving their teaching.

In short, faculty identified a lack of development plans to improve instruction in their institutions. They saw the process as providing only lip-service to meaningful evaluation. One faculty member suggested "firing all administrators who knew little or nothing or cared less about evaluation and quality education and replace with competent people." She then suggested creating an evaluation system that would "distinguish those minimally competent from those below minimal competence and provide remediation for the latter group with an outcome that would either (1) make them competent, or (2) permit their legal dismissal" (Licata and Andrews, 1992, p. 53).

Clearly evaluation is an important issue for faculty concerned about quality instruction. Faculty members are unhappy when they have to share teaching responsibilities within a department or division of the college with teaching colleagues they know are less than competent.

Faculty leaders have much at stake in the establishment of a solid and effective evaluation system. Licata and Andrews (1992) showed that faculty leaders were willing to articulate both the strengths and the weaknesses of college post-tenure evaluation in their colleges and made these recommendations:

- Tie evaluation systems to faculty development and to a formative purpose
- Provide incentives (merit for excellent performers)
- Train evaluators
- Ensure a systematic and consistent plan
- Make evaluation more effective in retention, dismissal, and reward
- Decrease frequency of evaluation

Many community colleges use student evaluation. Centra (1979) found students to be generally lenient in their judgment; thus, reliance on student evaluation may be misleading as to the effectiveness of some teachers. Centra quoted from a 1975 Educational Testing Service study showing that only 12 percent of 400,000 teachers in a national sample were rated below average in student reviews. Centra found that peers (teachers evaluating each other) were more lenient than student reviewers.

Cashin (1983) was critical of student evaluations and said students were not qualified as experts on whether an instructor was knowledgeable in his or her field of study. Cashin (1983) also reviewed twenty-two years of court cases and was unable to find a single case where a faculty member who was dismissed had student evaluation as a significant factor in leading to that dismissal. This study surely raised significant doubt relative to the legal considerations.

There is no other area of the college that will do more to ensure the excellence sought by the dean, president, and board of trustees than a high-quality and legally defensible faculty evaluation system.

Qualifications Handbook. A gap in the development of community college standards exists in several areas. None is more obvious than in the identification of requirements for teaching in various areas of the curriculum. Indeed, requirements and competency levels are much better defined at the elementary and secondary school levels. The academic dean of the college can have a major role in working with faculty to identify exactly what qualifications are required to teach in various degree and certificate programs. The dean can also identify qualifications necessary to teach specific courses. The outcome will be a clearly defined set of qualifications to guide the college in hiring faculty.

Mackey and Andrews (1983, p. 71) explored how the new tenure law for community colleges, adopted in 1981 in Illinois, could be used to improve instruction. The law outlined expectations for tenure but left key terms undefined. Illinois Valley Community College, working with the faculty, defined the following terms as a way of improving both their hiring and faculty evaluation processes:

Qualified—The term used to designate the minimum preparation level necessary for teaching employees to be hired for a specific area of instruction at the college.

Competent—The term used to refer to a employee who has both the minimum preparation level and has successfully undergone the tenure evaluation system of the college and/or has successfully prepared for and taught individual courses.

Competencies—The term used to spell out the exact areas of competence of a faculty member.

The *Qualifications Handbook* (1994) at Illinois Valley Community College provided a process for the college dean and department heads to determine whether faculty should be moved from a status of qualified to competent in the courses they taught. Knight (1983) stressed how important it was for division chairpersons to work with their faculty in developing the evaluation process. The process spelled out how individual faculty members could add to their competencies by preparing for and teaching new courses they were qualified to teach. This process applied to both non-tenured and tenured faculty.

Faculty members were highly involved in developing the evaluation process. They had to come to agreement with academic administrators in defining those basic qualifications.

A locally developed qualifications handbook can serve as a major tool for setting the standards for the college when no standards or documents are available at the state level for defining the terms *qualified, competent,* and *competencies* for two-year college instructors. It also provides a guarantee to faculty that their colleagues are well qualified and competent.

Recognition versus Merit Pay. Stevens, Goodwin, and Goodwin (1991) surveyed faculty in three types of colleges and found that 40 percent reported that their colleges did not "reward good teaching." Another 40 percent of the respondents reported a lack of "incentives supporting good teaching."

Merit pay is considered a financial award for outstanding faculty. It becomes part of a faculty member's base pay and raises that person beyond other faculty members in the same institution. Low pay has been one of the main factors causing faculty associations and unions not to want to see a small number of faculty obtain the majority of the funds that might be available for raises in any given year. Merit recognition, on the other hand, allows the best faculty to gain recognition, plaques, and sometimes a small one-time monetary award. This has become an acceptable outcome of faculty evaluation in a growing number of two-year colleges.

Few other issues create more havoc than rewarding faculty through merit pay as part of their base salary. A few years ago, while I was speaking on merit recognition for faculty at the American Community College Trustees (ACCT) annual meeting, the topic of merit pay came up. Trustees from three different colleges responded to my question asking who at the meeting represented colleges that had merit pay systems. Two respondents backed off quickly to my follow-up question: "Are they working effectively?" The third trustee continued to support the need for merit pay for two-year college faculty. Probing further, I found that the faculty were very unhappy with the system and the college did not have a sound evaluation system in place. That trustee admitted that it was far from being a panacea and that, "Yes, we are considering dumping it!"

Recognition for outstanding teaching has been found wanting in many community colleges. A national study by Andrews (1988) of two-year colleges found a small number of colleges with motivational recognition programs that worked. The successful programs had the following key core elements:

They were outgrowths of faculty evaluation systems conducted primarily by instructional administrators.
They avoided the merit pay issues by offering the alternative of merit recognition to outstanding faculty.
The faculty, administrators, and trustees found them to be acceptable.

Andrews (1993) noted that the number of community colleges reporting merit recognition plans in a nineteen-state region of the United States had risen from 55 to 166 between 1984–1985 and 1990–1991. Clearly, this is a good increase; nevertheless, many colleges still do not have recognition programs for their outstanding faculty members.

Conclusion

This chapter has focused on the role of the dean in community colleges and the relationship of the dean to the faculty. This role is challenging and demanding—and has many rewards. There is no greater reward for a dean than developing a highly competent faculty.

The importance of high-quality policies developed by the board of trustees should not be underestimated. The college president and board of trustees can be major sources of support for the dean when tough decisions have to be made. The dean and faculty will benefit from a well-developed and legally defensible evaluation system. Faculty should be involved in the development of the system. Their participation ensures that faculty development programs, recognition for outstanding teaching, and improvement plans and sanctions for unproductive faculty members will be supported by the faculty as a whole.

The dean must be competent, trusted, consistent, have integrity, and have an ability to resolve problems. These personal traits, teaching experiences, and hard work will move the institution into producing the kind of campus climate that highlights teaching and student learning.

References

Andrews, H. A. "Merit Recognition: The Acceptable Alternative." *ACCT Quarterly*, 1988, *12*(3), 24–27.

Andrews, H. A. "Expanding Merit Recognition Programs in Community Colleges." *Community College Review*, 1993, *20*(5), 50–58.

Andrews, H. A. *Teachers Can Be Fired: The Quest for Quality*. Chicago: Catfeet Press, 1995.

Cashin, W. E. "Concerns About Using Student Ratings in Community Colleges." In A. Smith (ed.), *Evaluating Faculty and Staff*. New Directions for Community Colleges, no. 41. San Francisco: Jossey-Bass, 1983.

Centra, J. A. *Determining Faculty Effectiveness*. San Francisco: Jossey-Bass, 1979.

Educational Testing Service. *Comparative Data Guide-Student Instructional Report*. Princeton, N.J.: Educational Testing Service, 1975.

Illinois Valley Community College. *Qualifications Handbook*. Oglesby, Ill.: Illinois Valley Community College, 1994.

Knight, J. H. "Developing a Qualifications Handbook: The Division Chairperson's Role." *Journal of Staff, Program and Organization Development*, 1983, *5*(2), 51–56.

Licata, C. M., and Andrews, H. A. "Faculty Leaders' Responses to Post-Tenure Evaluation Practices." *Community/Junior College Quarterly*, 1992, *16*, 47–56.

Mackey, B., and Andrews, H. A. "Reductions in Force in Higher Education." *Journal of Staff, Program, and Organization Development*, 1983, *1*, 69–72.

Marzano, W., and Andrews, H. A. "Meeting the Looming Faculty Shortage: Development from Within." *AACJC Journal*, 1990–1991, *61*(3).

Stevens, E., Goodwin, L., and Goodwin, W. "How Are We Different? Attitudes and Perceptions of Teaching Across Three Institutions." *Journal of Staff, Program, and Organization Development*, 1991, *9*(2), 69–82.

HANS A. ANDREWS is president of Olney Central College in Illinois, following eighteen years as dean of instruction at Illinois Valley Community College.

4

*When the college president and dean develop a close
working relationship, they act synergistically for the good
of the institution.*

The Dean and the President

Hans J. Kuss

The president and the chief academic officer (CAO) must have a special
relationship. It does not have to be personally close, but it must be professionally connected. In the context of this chapter, the CAO might be a vice
president or dean, depending on the size or the organizational title structure of the institution.

Too often, the president and CAO make the assumption that each acts
independently of the other. This assumption diminishes the synergy that
could be created if they worked together to develop a framework for action
focused on improvement. Several years ago, I read about the successes of
Northeastern Missouri State University. The president at that time was
Charles McClain. Whenever President McClain met with his CAO, he posed
the question, "Are *we* making a difference?"

Communication between the president and the CAO is essential.
Wheatley (1992) writes that employees rank poor communications at the
top of all major issues facing organizations. She states further that poor communication is a superficial diagnosis. In fact, we suffer from "a fundamental misperception of information: what it is, how it works, and what we
might expect from it" (p. 101). Therefore, a president and CAO must understand institutional goals and direction, and they must be in agreement with
and consistent about information they impart.

In my experience, presidents, especially new presidents, may find
intramural posturing, particularly from their immediate reports. Administrators from student services, business affairs, and academic affairs may initially concur with a new president's direction and communicate the
"refreshing" ideas to deans and chairpersons, but perhaps not in the way
that the president intended. A president can determine how and what is
communicated by reading minutes from division and department meetings.

Depending on their management style, presidents may see their administrative staff as separate entities or as members of a team, but rarely do they see the staff as extensions of themselves. From my experience, the president who sees those who report to him or her as extensions will think and speak in terms of "we." As the word *we* appears more and more in the president's language, others are encouraged to embrace the concept. The use of "we" enhances mutual trust, respect, and reliance. The language we use with our direct reports influences our behavior. Vaughan (1986) cites data that only 28 percent of presidents rely on the CAO as the primary confidant. This percentage is very low when one considers that the core of the mission of an educational institution is teaching and learning. Therefore, the president's extension of himself or herself as a coupled entity with the CAO is weak at best in most educational institutions.

As Wolverton (1984) observes, presidents and CAOs need to be "in philosophical and pragmatic agreement at least 80–85 percent of the time" (p. 143). It is essential, however, that some of the tough decisions that need to be made rest within that 80 to 85 percent. Although most presidents expect some disagreement, they also expect that their decisions will be carried forward as a "we" decision.

The president has the primary job of creating a platform from which actions take place, establishing goals toward which actions tend, creating standards to which actions rise, and contributing a tone by which all actions are characterized. In this regard, the CAO must understand a president's philosophy, motivation, directions, and actions. It is incumbent on the president to take the time to discuss these elements, strategies, and reasons with the CAO, who can then reinforce the communication that filters from the institution. The CAO has the responsibility for ensuring that the definitions within the president's communication are concise and consistent. Accordingly, the "Are we making a difference?" approach can be achieved only if the president and CAO are in sync philosophically and strategically.

Some presidents strive for a leadership team; others continue to use a dictatorial approach. The latter group knows all the words, but their actions are devoid of inclusion. The first step toward successful participatory management is forthright communication.

Communication Between CAO and President

Communication rifts between the CAO and the president begin in a number of ways. When the president finds fault with the CAO's plans and implementation strategies or is otherwise critical toward him or her, the CAO may refrain from asking the president how the rift occurred. Moreover, when a president condescends or finds fault, most colleagues will refute a "we" relationship and go along with a president until one of them leaves the institution. Nevertheless, the ultimate outcome of communication rifts causes

CAOs to be less forthcoming and candid. Presidents have a huge responsibility to encourage, and thus to empower, collegial trust.

Presidents can empower collegial trust by obtaining the context of statements made by CAOs. Too often, reactions by presidents to things heard cause the eventual rifts in presidential-CAO relationships. That is, a communication incongruence becomes elevated when values and strategies remain undefined between the two. Presidents can foster trust by seeking an understanding with their CAO.

To avoid a communication wedge between the president and the CAO, a president must, when confronted with a difference in philosophy or definition, ask, "How can *we* make that work?" During the course of my administrative tenure, whenever I was confronted with huge differences of opinion, style, or direction from CAOs, deans, or staff, this question caused both parties to share deeper understanding. "How can we make that work?" causes one to walk in the other person's shoes because more information comes forward and greater possibilities arise. In fact, a learning moment usually occurs when differences are examined openly rather than discovered.

Communication to the College Community

The CAO can serve as a confidant only if he or she can communicate from the platform established by the president. A CAO who is philosophically opposed to a particular initiative may communicate something other than the intent of the president. Problems also arise when the president does not take the time to explain or assumes that the CAO understands presidential inventiveness, responsibilities, and tasks to implement a given initiative. A common mishap occurs when the CAO says, "It's what the president wants," rather than, "We think this is best for the institution because . . ."

Often, and understandably, presidents cannot be as forthcoming as they would like because they have learned that they must think and communicate strategically. I know presidents who have had the experience that their statements have been misconstrued and reported to the board of trustees. This information, of course, can be one-sided and out of context, and consequently may place the president at odds with the trustees.

Faculty are keenly aware when a president and CAO are at odds because it is reflected in communication. Some faculty seem to relish the notion of driving a wedge into the president-CAO relationship by exacerbating the differences in what has been stated by either party. At times, communication differences may result in the president's distancing himself or herself from the CAO. The CAO can then never expect to be the president's confidant again.

Perhaps one of the most essential tasks of a CAO is to ensure that new academic programs are developed and old ones dismantled or eliminated, especially when old programs have saturated the market. At one institution an environmental science program has been in existence for six years. Two faculty members were hired to teach, promote, and articulate this program. But the number of graduates has declined steadily over six years, and only one student has graduated from the program every year for the past three years. A CAO's role affinity with the faculty may dissuade him or her from eliminating such a program. Moreover, most negotiated agreements contain provisos that ensure viable programs and eliminate those that do not have sufficient student enrollment. Too often, however, academic programs are optioned into other low-enrolled programs to bolster two or three dismal programs, an approach that provides only a temporary solution. A CAO's fear and avoidance of faculty uproar over program elimination is understandable, but it occurs only when an improper communication strategy is employed. In formal and informal ways, the president and CAO can present and seek information and communicate student concerns, employer interest, and employer statistics. Both parties can discuss a program's health. This should occur several times by strategic design so that if institutional support is severed, faculty will be prepared. In my experience, faculty members will not save bankrupt programs if they have been involved with fact finding about program need. A CAO who has the courage to work with faculty through such turbulent times gains considerable respect.

Fostering the Relationship

When CAOs refrain from exercising their responsibilities, presidents will assume them or assign them to someone else. And when CAOs find themselves disconnected from the strategic direction of the president, the presidents will locate another confidant in the institution. If a confidant is unavailable, presidents tend to keep their own counsel. The CAO position is one of the most essential positions in the institution, and most presidents fill this position with a person who will exercise leadership responsibility.

The relationship between the president and the CAO can be characterized as a set of rules:

The president must always be honest with the CAO, and the CAO must always be honest with the president.

The president must know the CAO both professionally and personally, and understand his or her strengths and weaknesses. The president must know what motivates the CAO, what causes fear and joy in this person, and what the CAO expects the institution to be in five to ten years. As well, CAOs need to know the president professionally and personally.

CAOs must never offer their loyalty to the president as if it were pocket change. Presidents must earn loyalty from faculty and staff.

Both president and CAO must work from the mission. This kind of work allows for building a "we" relationship. The mission can be the most important vehicle for building a collegial relationship.

A CAO's responsibility should be consistent with the president's framework for action. Thus, a CAO must determine whether the president is in a building or maintenance mode. The bridges that need to be constructed by both parties should be constructed around the framework of building or maintaining, or both, if need be. The former is riskier than the latter. It will serve an institution well if both parties operate from a building framework. The synergy realized from such a connected framework leads to institutional successes.

CAO Responsibilities

The CAO must ensure that meaningful new programs are developed and old ones eliminated. In addition, he or she must secure the use of technology in the classroom, find creative ways to help both full-time and part-time faculty engage in meaningful professional development activities, and encourage grant-writing initiatives. When CAOs engage in redundant or routine tasks (course schedules, equipment bidding and purchases), they diminish their importance to the president and their value to the mission of the institution. Routine tasks should be assigned at the division level.

Bennis (1989) suggests that many of us "find ourselves acting on routine problems because they are the easiest things to handle. We hesitate to get involved too early in the bigger ones—we collude, as it were, in the unconscious conspiracy to immerse us in routine." The tendency not to "push up the tough decisions" rests in the fact that many administrators would rather manage than lead because "they do not want to take the responsibility for or bear the consequences of decisions they properly should make" (p. 17).

Finding ways to maintain faculty motivation and promote risk taking and growth are important CAO functions. The president and CAO must work together to ensure the advancement of institutional goals. They must communicate institutional goals and how they relate at the department or division level. The weakest area in most institutions occurs at the division or department chair level, because most chairpersons come to the position without preparation, work in relative isolation from each other, and often serve with inadequate support. Yet the position of chairperson has grown significantly over the past two decades. Chairpersons are responsible for scheduling, part-time faculty hiring, evening class schedules, and sometimes faculty professional development. Since many administrators recognize the lack of preparedness of chairpersons, CAOs and presidents must find ways to impart institutional goals and strategies to their division heads.

Here too communication can be difficult. Chairpersons are generally closer to faculty than to CAOs. Consequently, they may tend to construct and filter information so that it is more palatable to the faculty. At times, palatability is inconsistent with the tough decisions required by the president. Reading division minutes can give presidents and CAOs insight into how information was communicated and understood.

Division or department meetings hosted by the CAO can provide valuable clues to a president. To be sure, a president can inquire about any strategic direction of those who participate in meetings held by the CAO. This is not a matter of spying; it is more a matter of taking the temperature of the institution to measure its readiness to move in a given direction. From this measurement, the president can also determine whether to provide more information and how to communicate it. More than just being supportive, the CAO must bring connectivity to the president's agenda; otherwise, the institution will not move forward as quickly.

Conclusion

Both the president and the CAO have the responsibility for developing the strategic agenda for the institution. A shared vision should be the foundation on which they build their framework for action. According to Senge (1990), "A vision is truly shared when you and I have a similar picture and are committed to one another having it, not just to each of us, individually, having it. When people truly share a vision they are connected, bound together by a common aspiration" (p. 206). It is the connection by common aspiration that will maximize leadership synergies.

Presidents and CAOs should couple their communication and management methodology to maximize their leadership possibilities. They must construct an understanding not only around what has occurred and what will occur, but also around whether improvement has occurred and what they can do to cause improvement. Through the construction, the president and CAO can achieve the "we" necessary to lead synergistically.

Generally a president looks for a CAO who complements his or her management style and vision. Communication provides the avenue for determining how they can cooperate with each other in the best interest of the college. Presidents who are deeply introspective should know their limitations and get people around them who complement their strengths and weaknesses. The president and CAO should work together to set the metaphorical table around their strengths with the china and silverware of improvement and understanding.

References

Bennis, W. *Why Leaders Can't Lead.* San Francisco: Jossey-Bass, 1989.
Senge, P. M. *The Fifth Discipline.* New York: Doubleday Currency, 1990.
Vaughan, G. B. *The Community College Presidency.* New York: American Council on Education/Macmillan, 1986.
Wheatley, M. J. *Leadership and the New Science.* San Francisco: Berrett-Koehler, 1992.
Wolverton, R. E. In E. B. Ehrle and J. B. Bennett (eds.), *Managing the Academic Enterprise: Case Studies for Deans and Provosts.* New York: American Council on Education/Macmillan, 1988.

HANS J. KUSS serves as president of Maysville Community College, Maysville, Kentucky. Prior to this position, he served as dean of arts and sciences at Triton College, River Grove, Illinois; dean of instruction at Garden City Community College, Garden City, Kansas City; and regional dean of academic affairs at Ivy Tech State College, Indiana.

5

Many of the academic manager's decisions have far-reaching consequences, having an impact on more individuals than those initially involved. This chapter outlines five aspects that deans should consider when making sensitive, difficult decisions.

Aspects of Difficult Decisions

George L. Findlen

The visibility of the academic dean, whether that person is the chief academic officer or the middle management division dean in larger institutions, makes decision making a lonely activity. Reactions to decisions come quickly, and the entire institution, especially a smaller one, is likely to know what the dean decides. Criticism, when it comes, is almost immediate. If the decision is made hurriedly in the press of daily business, it may be unwise and lessen a dean's followership among faculty (Kelley, 1992). Academic deans should acquire a habit of examining the aspects of difficult situations before making a decision.

A Sampling of Difficult Situations

Look at a few of those situations that make deans say, "What do I do now?"

The Parking Lot Incident

You enter your office one balmy Monday morning in July and are greeted by the campus security officer. He hands you a complaint filed by a student last Friday afternoon. The student was having difficulty making a left-hand turn into heavy traffic as she was leaving the parking lot. An impatient driver behind her honked his pickup truck horn and leaned out of his window to yell an obscenity at her. The student recognized him as one of her summer session instructors.

The access lane from the parking lot to the county highway is county land, not college land.

You present the instructor with a copy of the complaint and make a copy for the faculty grievance representative as required by the faculty union contract. Upon receiving his copy, the faculty grievance representative warns you

that if you act on the complaint in any way, he will take the issue to arbitration. Your personnel director, a timid man for whom avoidance of conflict is
all-important, agrees with the faculty grievance representative. Unfortunately,
the college has no professional ethics policy. Do you seek to discipline the
instructor for his unprofessional behavior?

An Angry Parent

You pick up the telephone one afternoon and hear a parent complain about
how one of your instructors is teaching an Introduction to Psychology course.
The complaint is about the instructor's choice of exercises for getting students
to apply Kohlberg's stages of moral development to themselves. The instructor asked students to put themselves in the position of a doctor whose ter-
minally ill cancer patient had but a few days to live and was asking the doctor
to help her end her life. Students were to think of a response, then identify
where they would fit on Kohlberg's continuum. The parent, a nurse, accuses
the instructor of teaching students to commit euthanasia.

Everything you recall about academic freedom fills your mind. As you
open your mouth to explain that, you remember a situation in which a member of the college's board of trustees lambasted you for how the nursing
instructors processed students who failed a major test twice. Not wanting a
repeat of that confrontation, you hesitate. Do you defend your instructor's
academic freedom to the parent?

An Angry Writing Student

On returning to your office complex after a meeting, your secretary catches
your eye and says that a student is waiting to see you with a complaint. You
introduce yourself to an angry middle-aged man and usher him into your
office. Before you can sit, he blurts out that his writing instructor humiliates
him by requiring him to participate in small group discussions of class writing, that he is funded by the Department of Vocational Rehabilitation, and
that the college has to accommodate him. He demands to have all assignments given to him to do by himself at home. In fact, he demands that he not
have to attend class at all, and he insists that he will go straight to the president if you do not agree immediately.

You are taken aback by his aggressiveness. You hesitate to call the college's Americans with Disabilities Act (ADA) specialist because that person
has consistently advocated for whatever special students ask, even when
opposed by reasonable faculty. Does the ADA permit an instructor to require
participation in small group work in a writing class?

An Anxious Faculty Member

On a quiet day during spring break, one of your new instructors, a timid person, knocks on your door and asks if she may speak with you. She speaks with

hesitation and describes several events, all recent. One day late in the afternoon, she looked up from her office desk and saw an older male instructor standing in the hall looking at her; he quickly walked away when she looked up. Earlier in the week, the same instructor showed up in the cafeteria serving line just behind her; she had not noticed him walking behind her. On the last day of class before break, she walked into one of her classes and found him there; he introduced her to her class with a circus-like flourish and left without speaking to her. After sharing several more odd events with you, she shivers and expresses concern that he may be stalking her. She hastens to add that she does not want to "get him into trouble" and finishes by asking what she should do.

What do you say to her? More important, what do you do?

Any of these situations has the potential to end in an angry confrontation in the president's office, before an arbiter, or even in a federal court. All require careful forethought; some call for research and consultation.

The Five Aspects of a Problem

When something complicated comes up, wise deans should examine five aspects of the problem before acting.

Problems. The first aspect of a difficult or controversial situation is the problem itself. Experience suggests that the presenting problem is almost always the behavior of the person complained about or a solution the complaining person wants. "I don't like so-and-so's teaching" is an example of the former; "Why won't you have a fit before the vice president and get us more money?" is an example of the latter. To uncover the root problem, ask yourself, "What is the complaining person's unmet need?" Fisher and Ury (1981) refer to this as focusing on interests, not on positions.

In the case of the student leaving the parking lot, the presenting problem is the instructor's behavior; the root problem is the student's desire for dignity and respect, particularly from college employees in positions of authority. In the same case, the union's presenting problem is the supervisor's exercise of authority over off-campus, after-hours faculty behavior; its root interest is to control administrators and minimize bargaining member accountability. For the angry parent, the presenting problem is the instructor's alleged encouragement of students to commit euthanasia; the underlying problem is anxiety over the effect of a secular institution on a parent's desire to shape the values of her now-adult child. For the angry writing student, the presenting problem is an instructor's class requirement; underneath, the problem is fear of failure in a setting more demanding than his skill level can handle and comfort level permits. In the stalking case, the presenting problem is the male faculty member's behavior; the root problem is a need for emotional safety.

Defining the problem is important; otherwise, the dean will grapple with the wrong issues.

Issues. The second aspect of a problem situation is what must be determined to be fact. At the outset, a dean must determine who said or did what. The task may require seeking the president's counsel and may require looking up the pertinent law or policy. The *Grievance Guide* (1995) and Bickel and Brechner's *The College Administrator and the Courts* (1988) are but two useful resources that administrators should have available for ready reference. (See Chapter Ten in this volume for other resources that academic managers can turn to when making difficult decisions.) To get at the issues, ask, "What fundamental, yes-no questions must be answered?" Think of the issue as the allegations that must be confirmed or the policies that must be applied correctly.

In the parking lot incident, the dean must find out whether faculty can be disciplined for off-hours behavior off college property when that behavior affects the ability of the college to fulfill its mission. The upset parent's complaint requires that the dean first determine with some accuracy exactly what took place during the class exercise. Who determines what is to be taught in a college classroom and how it is to be taught is treated amply in the literature. It is important, however, to consider whether the exercise fosters or impedes student learning. A closely related issue is what kind of relationship a publicly supported college seeks with the taxpaying parents of its students. In the case of the angry writing student, the issue to be resolved is whether the ADA permits a faculty member to require group work in a writing class for students whose mental faculties make that difficult. A related issue is whether the program the student is enrolled in has identified "ability to work with others" as an essential function of the program. For the anxious faculty member, the first issue is whether the events she described have in fact taken place in the manner described. The second issue is whether the college's policies deal with the alleged behavior.

Not identifying all relevant issues may lead a dean to ignore a key individual.

Players. No administrator acts in a vacuum. All colleges have constituencies, and all constituencies have some influence if not power. For this aspect, ask two questions. "Who, other than the person making the complaint and the person complained about, have a stake or interest in the situation?" and "What effect on the administrator can these two players have?" This aspect of a case involves being aware of the context, which is different at every institution.

In the parking lot case, the other players include at least the union grievance representative and possibly arbitrators in the state. Include the public; complaining students talk widely, and egregious offenses not dealt with reach wider audiences. In a small institution having a board that takes an interest in the smallest operational details, the dean may even have to think of a board member and the president. In the case of the offended parent, the public is a player, and the college's reputation is potentially at risk. Again, if the college community is small, there is a possibility of board involvement. Depending on what kind of relationship exists between the administration and faculty, the dean may deal with the union grievance representative as well. In the case of the angry writing student, the players include the special populations counselor and possibly the administrators above the dean. In the case of the anxious faculty member, the other players may include a woman's support group, if the college has one, and the individual responsible for investigating sexual harassment complaints. Administrators ignore these unseen players at their peril.

Options. For any problem, administrators must think of alternative courses of action and select the wisest, most effective one consistent with fairness and the college's mission. It involves traditional brainstorming. Think of this aspect in terms of two questions. "What alternative courses of action are available to the administrator?" and "What is the foreseeable effect of each option?" Wise administrators look for courses of action that deal with the surface problem as well as the underlying one, and they often seek counsel.

In the parking lot incident, there are two major issues the dean must reckon with, and it may simplify matters to separate them. One issue is what the dean does for the student's need for dignity. Noel Levitz Centers' *Connections* (1993) teaches staffers to put themselves in the students' place and apologize for those students' negative experience. That is an inexpensive and quickly done course of action for an administrator who speaks for an academic unit or college. The other issue involves what the dean will do regarding the faculty member's unprofessional behavior. If the president or chief academic officer will not support disciplining the faculty member with a written reprimand, the dean can at least give an oral reprimand or a memo describing the conversation held between the administrator and faculty member that does not get into the faculty member's official personnel file. In the case of the angry parent, the dean may be able to set up a meeting of the parent with the faculty member. That solution would enable the dean to support academic freedom while acknowledging the need of the parent to present her beliefs and ascertain for herself what took place in her daughter's classroom. It may be that there are relevant college policies that the dean can send to her detailing student rights and the college's complaint procedure. Certainly the dean should commit to checking her allegations by visiting with the instructor and calling the parent with the findings.

In the case of the angry student, the dean should call the college's special populations counselor or coordinator to confirm that the student indeed has a documented disability and review what the ADA requires. A meeting with the student at which the special populations counselor attends is certainly in order.

The anxious faculty member requires that the dean reread the college's sexual harassment policy and seek to confirm the events as described. One option is to trigger the college's sexual harassment complaint policy. Another is to meet privately with the faculty member to discuss the behavior and ask that it stop. The more options there are, the better. What will work at one college may not at another due to organizational climate, institutional policy, and a host of other variables.

Principles. For everything humans do, there is a motive and there is a goal, however vaguely understood. At best, that motive is a basic principle. The popularity of Stephen Covey's *Seven Habits* (1989) is rooted in the human hunger for core principles to guide action. Principles are the major rules of life, rooted in the concepts behind federal and state laws, major concepts like justice, and the core concepts of effective leadership. Ultimately, principles are wisdom. To get at a principle, ask, "What rule can you cite that should guide the administrator?"

In the case of the parking lot incident, the principle is that all students have a right to be treated decently by all employees of the college, both on and off the property and during and after work hours. Moreover, a college's administration has a right to demand that its employees treat students and each other with dignity.

In the case of the angry parent, there are at least two principles. The first is that the faculty member has the academic freedom to determine effective ways of guiding student learning of legitimate curricular subject matter. The second is that taxpaying parents of adult students have a right to ask colleges they support to be accountable, which includes listening to their concerns and making known college policies. In the case of the angry student, the principle is that a faculty member has the right to require student participation in learning activities that faculty commonly use to assist student learning. (The ADA requires removing barriers to student participation in education; it does not require the removal of reasonable requirements.) However, students have a right to complain and to have their complaint heard. In the case of the anxious faculty member, the principle I come up with is that all employees have a right to emotional security.

Conclusion

The press of daily business, especially in merged or downsized organizations in which a single administrator supervises fifty to one hundred full-time faculty members and another fifty to one hundred part-time faculty members, often makes it difficult to have the time to think through any of these aspects, much less each of them. Wise administrators always have a colleague to share problems with. Martin and Samels (1997) call for regional networks of chief academic officers. A colleague with a willing ear within the college or at a nearby college is a godsend for sorting out difficult challenges. Used thoughtfully, these five aspects provide academic managers with a useful heuristic for thinking through problems.

References

Bickel, R. and Brechner, J. *The College Administrator and the Courts.* Asheville, N.C.: College Administration Publications, 1988.

Connections: Practice for Excellence, Path to Success. (Rev. 3rd ed.) Bloomington, Minn.: Noel Levitz Centers, 1993.

Covey, S. R. *The Seven Habits of Highly Successful People: Restoring the Character Ethic.* New York: Simon & Schuster, 1989.

Fisher, R., and Ury, W. *Getting to Yes: Negotiating Agreement Without Giving In.* New York: Penguin Books, 1981.

Grievance Guide. (9th ed.) Washington, D.C.: Bureau of National Affairs, 1995.

Kelley, R. E. *The Power of Followership: How to Create Leaders People Want to Follow and Followers Who Lead Themselves.* New York: Doubleday, 1992.

Martin, J., Samels, J. E., and others. *First Among Equals.* Baltimore: Johns Hopkins University Press, 1997.

GEORGE L. FINDLEN *is the dean of general education and educational services at Western Wisconsin Technical College. He and his colleague, Rose Ann Findlen, a vice president of student services at Madison Area Technical College, consult with two-year colleges, leading case study workshops on problems that instructional administrators face.*

6

"Conflict IS the job," the seasoned administrator tells his younger colleague. But conflict may offer opportunities as well as obstacles and ought not be avoided.

Conflict: The Skeleton in Academe's Closet

Rose Ann Findlen

Recently two college administrators, one near retirement and the other early in his administrative career, spoke in the hall. The junior administrator complained bitterly about how exhausting and time-consuming it was to deal constantly with conflicts at work. He mourned that he could not do the important, transformational educational work that he had been hired to do. "No, Dave," the senior administrator said to him gently and sadly. "Conflict IS the job. To think otherwise is to delude yourself."

Seasoned administrators have experienced conflicts between students and faculty, students and administrators, and among students many times. Emotionally, some feel comfortable with their own institutional policies and with their own problem-solving skills; they accept fully that a substantial, regrettably necessary, part of their jobs is to manage conflict. Prospective administrators, on the other hand, are universally shocked and dismayed to find that this role is not only going to be a substantial part of their jobs but that it is also going to be much more emotionally draining and legally sensitive than they had ever imagined.

Gentle deans puffing on imported, scented tobacco in Meerschaum pipes and wearing leather patches on their well-worn Scottish tweed jackets will be eaten alive in the litigious environment in which today's college administrators work. Not only must they cope with a less civil higher education environment, but they must also stay abreast of increasingly complex legal issues relating to a host of possible sources of conflict: Americans with Disabilities Act, affirmative action, sexual harassment, freedom of speech, academic freedom, and the rights of diverse student and faculty populations. Philip K. Howard, in *The Death of Common Sense* (1994), documents our society's increasing treatment of special interests as "constitutional rights." For college administrators, these legal complexities present additional demands on their knowledge, skills, and abilities in their management of conflict.

The novice administrator's wistful hope that he could spend the bulk of his time on mission-central, educationally transforming activities is indicative of his and others' belief in a set of myths surrounding conflict.

Three Myths About Conflict

Myth 1: Conflict is avoidable. Really good leaders so inspire their followers that conflict does not arise. Sightings of gracious exchanges among academics strolling across a quiet, grassy campus with the carillon tolling in the background are as likely as reports of the abominable snowman eating lunch in the women's dorm. Nonetheless, many academics downplay the prevalence of conflict within higher education. Holton (1995) reports that whenever she discussed her research project on conflict in higher education, "academics almost always responded "Conflict? In higher education? Surely not!". . . There is a sense, often articulated, that because of the nature of the academy, conflict should be cloaked" (p. 1). A study by the Center for the Study of the Department Chair (Gmelch and Burns, 1991) indicates that chairs identified conflict with their colleagues as their major source of stress. In identifying sources of job dissatisfaction, the chairs identified interpersonal conflict as being second only to bureaucratic red tape and paperwork. Holton argues that the reality of conflict in higher education must be acknowledged and, to maintain the essence of academia itself, educators must learn principles and practices of conflict management.

The pervasiveness of confrontational interactions in higher education, whether from students or from faculty members, saps the will of college administrators to enter into conflict. Over time, many become worn down and choose not to engage in necessary discussions and principled decision making within an anger-laden environment. Conflict exists at every level of higher education: from student life directors who are negotiating peace among ethnically diverse students to college boards that are setting policy. In California, the average tenure of two-year college presidents is two years; nationally, two-year institutions see a new president join the fray every five years. I know a well-known and highly respected college president who resigned from his post and returned to graduate teaching following a bruising eighteen-month court battle in which he had persevered in acting on both legal and moral principle; he lost on a technicality. His will to stand on principle at that institution was worn away.

Myth 2: Consensus-seeking team structures will eliminate conflict. Although the use of strategies to seek consensus is an important tool in conflict management, it is not a panacea. In fact, excessive consensus seeking may permit an environment in which individual interest groups gain veto power over a proposed action through refusing to reach consensus. The administrator who has publicly stated that the group will reach a consensus is hamstrung. Important educational decisions can be delayed by months or even years if the administrator misjudges the power of special interests within the team or naively hopes to avoid conflict and difficult decisions through exhortations to team spirit. By refusing to acknowledge the probability of conflict within the team, the administrator may hope to avoid pain, but may not adequately take into account the sources of conflict that underlie decisions and activities throughout higher education.

Myth 3: Feminine styles of leadership prevent conflict. Many articles make much of the power of "feminine styles of leadership" to reduce conflict, claiming that women leaders are better listeners and are more likely, by virtue of their role conditioning, to seek consensus and work in teams than men are. As such, the argument goes, women are well suited to the demands of leadership today. A respect for the views of others and a tendency to negotiate agreements rather than to rule by fiat are characteristics that often promote a resolution of conflict. This view, however, does not take into account the elements of conflict management that are difficult for many women and men to learn to deal with:

Conflict is inherent in organizations and, many times, healthy.
There is a time to listen but also a time to "know when to hold and know when to fold"; in other words, there are specific negotiation strategies to learn beyond team building.
Negotiation strategies include both soft and hard approaches. A seasoned administrator knows how to use both.

In training academic leaders to manage conflict, it is unwise to overemphasize the so-called feminine and masculine approaches to leadership. Rather, good conflict management skills encompass a variety of strategies and principles that transcend gender. Leaders of either sex can cause themselves undue angst by identifying particular responses to decision making or conflict resolution as "masculine" or "feminine"; a gender-based focus may prevent them from learning and using the full array of strategies available to them in managing conflict. For example, some beginning woman administrators struggle to come to terms with themselves and their gender role when they feel the pressure that others may see them as not being acceptably supportive. If they have had a traditional upbringing, they may feel that they are not "nice people" and that they have failed if they did not reach consensus; their sensitivity on this issue may prevent them from moving forward to manage the conflict effectively. Almost all human beings wish to be liked by others, although gender identity may exacerbate this issue for women. An emphasis on the full acceptable range of tools available to managers in managing conflict may liberate them from the constraints of gender stereotypes.

Sources of Conflict in Higher Education

In a report from the National Institute for Dispute Resolution, Folger and Shubert (1995) acknowledge that "colleges and universities are no longer seen as quiet enclaves free from the conflicts that arise in all hierarchical organizations. . . . Differences in goals or plans for the allocation of resources, misinterpretation or inconsistent application of institutional regulations, breaches of formal or informal contracts, power struggles and personal antagonisms are all possible sources of conflict" (p. 5). Anyone who has worked as a two-year college administrator knows the truth of this statement.

Administrators and Faculty. These conflicts take place within an organization where the traditional expectation has been that colleges are academic communities that "should transcend some of the internal struggles that characterize other organizations" (p. 5).

The root causes of conflict, then, are the same as those in any other complex organization; however, there are additional factors that contribute to conflict between instructional administrators and faculty. Holton and Phillips (1995) cite eight reasons that faculty members and administrators are frequently at odds:

1. Being an administrator is not a promotion for a faculty member, it is a new career path.
2. Faculty members and administrators answer to different authorities.
3. Policy is always in conflict with local options. The independence of the permanent, full-time faculty member is often an affront to the administrator.
4. There are persistent irritations—personality conflicts, jealousy, tenure and promotion decisions, hiring decisions, new courses, course assignments, policy, and, of course, parking.
5. Standards of judgment are never clear. Faculty members do not really understand how they are judged on teaching, service, and scholarship. The roles of student evaluation, peer evaluation, and evaluation by the higher-ups are not always clear.
6. Faculty members are urgent for input. That means they want their own way. Administrators want to give the illusion of input. That means they will have their own way and act like it was democratically decided.
7. It is rarely clear to either party how much power each has and how one can affect the other. The faculty member is a potential saboteur or guerilla. The administrator is an obstacle.
8. There are natural irritations in any boss-employee relationship, and despite protestations to the contrary, the administrator is a boss [pp. 44–49].

Gmelch and Burns (1991) found that 60 percent of chairs' sources of job dissatisfaction was attributable to engaging in conflict with faculty regarding the following issues:

- Interfaculty conflict
- Faculty attitude
- Unsupportive faculty
- Unsupportive chair
- Role of evaluation
- Role of mediation

These types of faculty-administrator disputes are particularly relevant in understanding any community college's culture. The stance that administrators and faculty take relative to each other around these issues dramatically affects the institutional climate, the college's educational effectiveness, and its integrity. Gmelch and Miskin (1993) assert that "nothing is as important for American higher education than the emergence of academic leaders equipped to handle conflict" (p. 103).

Students and Faculty. A second major area of conflict relates to student-faculty roles and relationships. Students seeking redress for their grievances, due process, and, sometimes, just a meaningful discussion relating to a conflict or controversy will state their case for justice or change within the context of existing conflicts or a conflict-avoidance culture at that institution. A particularly difficult conflict to negotiate for instructional administrators is balancing the rights and responsibilities of faculty against the obligation to ensure due process for students in academic matters. Tucker and Bryan (1988) identify common sources of conflict between faculty and students: requests for rule waivers, grade appeals, horror stories, race or sex discrimination complaints, poor teaching, and tasteless classroom conduct on the part of a faculty member.

In addition, students come to the instructional administrator's office with a considerable amount of dissatisfaction and high expectations for what the dean will do. When students bring their conflicts with faculty to instructional administrators, they frequently have attempted, without success, to resolve them with the faculty member directly or through an informal mediator such as a counselor. At this point, they feel extremely angry, disappointed, or desperate. George Findlen (1997) notes too that they bring a set of expectations with them about how authority figures work. In one authority paradigm, for example, students believe that the instructional administrator is a parent figure whose duty it is to decide the merits of the case and remedy the student's problem without further consultation. Students who feel powerless, and sometimes realistically, are looking for someone who has more power than the faculty member to help them. They have little or no awareness of the complicated relationship between the faculty member and the administrator.

The instructional administrator handling the student grievance against a faculty member is caught between a rock and a hard place. The inherent tensions that exist between faculty and their supervisors on an ongoing basis are forced to the surface by the student with a grievance. Within that dynamic, protestations to the contrary about the "student being first," the instructional administrators know that they will be in a work relationship with the faculty members for years to come, while students come and go.

An examination of the eight reasons for administrator-faculty conflict that Holton and Phillips listed reveals multiple sources of stress and tension for the administrator who is trying to address a student's complaint. A student who is asking an administrator to mediate a conflict regarding a faculty member's classroom conduct taps into all of the eight reasons:

1. The administrator is not a teacher.
2. The instructor and the administrator answer to different authorities.
3. The policy may be in conflict with the faculty member's exercise of a local option.
4. The conflict may have relevance to a persistent source of irritation between the two, such as a difference of opinion about course content.
5. Standards of judgment may not be clear—for example, what is gratuitous vulgar language versus the deliberate use of an example for instructional purposes.
6. The faculty believe they are not consulted enough or soon enough on these matters.
7. Each can potentially harm the other.
8. The administrator has positional power.

The instructional administrator experiences severe stress in balancing these sources of conflict against the rights of the students and his or her responsibility to the students.

New Approaches to Conflict

The traditional value placed on collegiality and community in academia continues to discourage an open recognition of the necessity for formalized training to prepare instructional administrators to manage conflict on the scale that has emerged in higher education. One reason that conflict is not recognized, much less dealt with skillfully, is that training on how to manage conflict is absent from graduate programs in educational administration. Conflict management training programs or formal dispute resolution consultation entities are now established at more than one hundred higher education institutions in the United States (Holton, 1995). Although such tools and strategies for helping college administrators effectively cope with conflict do exist, they are scattered and relatively inaccessible to administrators who are unaware of them or unable to attend. Systematic, sustained support for training college administrators to manage conflict effectively is rare in educational administration graduate programs and institutional staff development.

Staff development programs and graduate curricula for educational administrators focus on transformational leadership and the importance of optimism and proactivity in leading effectively. Contract management and educational supervision courses in prestigious programs focus on theoretical and structural issues. An examination of graduate course offerings at three prestigious universities offering graduate degrees in educational administration (the University of Michigan-Ann Arbor, UCLA, and the University of Wisconsin-Madison) reveals that none offers course-length preparation for conflict management in their departmental curricula. At Stanford University, James Lyons uses a series of in-box situations to heighten student services graduate students' awareness of communication strategies and legal issues relating to college students. In general, however, handling complaints and conflicts does not seem to be considered an important topic for systematic, sustained graduate study and practice in educational administration, undoubtedly because of its unabashed attention to method and practice rather than to theory and academics' desire to view higher education institutions as copacetic academic communities.

Understandably, too, few students or faculty wish to dwell on the dark side of the college administrator's role. Systematic, ongoing training in managing conflict is notably absent from professional educators' conferences and educational administrators' programs of study. Occasionally administrators attend short sessions on conflict resolution while at work or at conferences, but these brief exposures without structured practice will not create substantial change within individuals and institutions.

Poorly managed conflict drains the energies and wounds the hearts of more educators than we care to admit. Failure to understand how to prevent unmanaged or unresolved conflicts from reaching the courts leads the arbitrator or governing board to consume untold resources of college time and money. A colleague reminds me that "it is difficult to remember that the original goal was to drain the swamp when you're up to your hip boots in alligators!"

The conflict management skills of administrators are of paramount importance to the well-being of the institution and to higher education in general. In most institutions, however, this dimension of leadership and community building remains hidden, partly through lack of knowledge of conflict management and partly through a wish to adhere to the academic values that shaped so many at an earlier time.

To put the issue of conflict in higher education within a historical perspective, the notion that conflict is an important element to nurture and to use as a tool for positive change is relatively recent. Table 6.1 sets out three historical approaches to handling conflict.

Many academics are finding they are in cultural conflict with their colleagues about the notion of conflict. One set of traditionalist colleagues thinks that conflict is destructive and seeks to suppress it totally, while another set of colleagues operates from the stance of the principled approach and

Table 6.1. Approaches to Organizational Conflict

Period	Philosophy	Nature	Prescription Strategy
1890s–1940s	Traditional	Destructive	Eliminate
1950s–1980s	Behavioral	Natural	Accept
Present	Principled	Necessary	Encourage

Source: Gmelch and Miskin (1993, p. 106).

attempts to encourage conflict. A substantial number of higher education administrators still espouse the traditional approach to conflict while privately acknowledging the inherent nature of a complex and changing institution to be one of conflicted interactions.

In an increasingly challenging higher education environment, Holton (1995) notes that "we need a culture that supports and acknowledges a systemic view of conflict, a view that acknowledges that conflict within one part of the academy has an effect on all other parts. As systems theory purports, change and conflict permeate the entire system. And so dealing with the conflict will require an engagement of all the elements of the systems and a cultural shift for most institutions of higher education" (p. 93).

A comprehensive approach to conflict management training needs to encompass conflict management processes and practices, analyses of the types of conflict in higher education, and an application of sound pedagogical strategies for modeling, reinforcing, and internalizing conflict management skills. In addition, graduate assistantships, internships, and on-the-job staff development programs need to provide a mechanism for ongoing support and mentoring of staff members who frequently are engaged in managing conflict. Such a sustained organizational development approach to conflict management will improve the quality of discourse in academia, the integrity of decision making, the climate of the institution, and the effectiveness and well-being of the college administrator. A more honest and deliberate approach to conflict management through systematic training and ongoing support for applying conflict management principles could free college administrators to fulfill their higher education purposes more effectively.

In addition to the disillusionment that administrators often experience relating to conflict, colleges also suffer a loss of human potential and productivity through not addressing conflict issues squarely and systematically in their staff development and mentoring programs. One of my friends moved from a curriculum development staff position to an associate dean position two years ago. A few days ago, she called to say, "I'm looking for a new job. People here are so mean and ugly that I can't stand it. I got into this work to work with faculty and to improve education, not to deal with resistance and hard feelings all the time." Until my friend faces the inevitability of conflict, leans into the inevitability of pain, and develops a range of strategies for managing conflict, she will always, I fear, be looking for another job.

References

Findlen, G. "Student Complaint Paradigms." Paper presented at Kansas State University's National Academic Chairs' Conference, Orlando, Fla., 1997.

Folger, J., and Shubert, J. J. *Resolving Student-Initiated Grievances in Higher Education: Dispute Resolution Procedures in a Non-Adversarial Setting.* National Institute for Dispute Resolution Report, no. 3. Washington, D.C.: National Institute for Dispute Resolution, 1995.

Gmelch, W. H., and Burns, J. S. "Sources of Stress for Academic Department Chairs: A National Study." Paper presented at the American Educational Research Association Conference, Chicago, Apr. 1991. (ED 339 306)

Gmelch, W., and Miskin, V. *Leadership Skills for Department Chairs.* Bolton, Mass.: Anker Publishing Co., 1993.

Holton, S. (ed.). *Conflict Management in Higher Education.* New Directions for Higher Education, no. 92. San Francisco: Jossey-Bass, 1995.

Holton, S., and Phillips, G. "Can't Live with Them, Can't Live Without Them: Faculty and Administrators in Conflict." In S. Holton (ed.), *Conflict Management in Higher Education.* New Directions for Higher Education, no. 92. San Francisco: Jossey-Bass, 1995.

Howard, P. K. *The Death of Common Sense: How Law Is Suffocating America.* New York: Random House, 1994.

Tucker, A., and Bryan, R. *The Academic Dean: Dove, Dragon, and Diplomat.* New York: American Council on Education and Macmillan, 1988.

ROSE ANN FINDLEN *is vice president for student services at Madison Area Technical College in Madison, Wisconsin. She and her colleague, George Findlen, a dean of general education and educational services at Western Wisconsin Technical College, consult with two-year colleges, leading case study workshops on problems that instructional administrators face.*

7

Financial management is crucial not only to the dean's personal survival, but also to the survival of the entire institution. The chapter offers an introduction to the subject and nomenclature of finance.

Academic Economics: The Academic Dean and Financial Management

Susan A. McBride

"The age of accountability has opened as legislators and taxpayer groups are asking, 'How are educators spending our money?'"(Cohen, 1992, p. 34). Academic economics is a major concern of instructional administrators everywhere. Frequently faculty criticize academic administrators for being too concerned with money. Within that criticism is the often-unstated accusation that administrators are not concerned enough with the real issues of higher education, such as instructional quality. This accusation is often raised when faculty hear that class sizes must increase, that faculty workload is threatened, or that additional full-time faculty will not be hired. The serious academic dean finds such accusations troubling. However, there is no way to get around the fact that the amount of money available to community colleges is limited. Deans must work hard to see that their institution gets as much money as possible and that it is spent effectively.

Deans are generally not prepared for their financial management roles. Research by Anderson (1973) indicates that deans report that while their formal academic preparation familiarized them with teaching, learning, and curriculum issues, it did not provide adequate coverage of budgets and budgeting issues. In similar research over twenty years later, Townsend and Bassoppo-Moyo (1996) found that for academic deans, the area most desired for additional technical competence was in budgeting and finance, leading them to recommend that higher education doctoral programs should offer courses in budget and finance.

Traditional academic leaders had to think strategically, remove obstacles, develop ownership, and take self-directed actions to move their institutions ahead. To these qualities today's leaders must add the ability to think

NEW DIRECTIONS FOR COMMUNITY COLLEGES, no. 109, Spring 2000 © Jossey-Bass Publishers intuitively, take risks, assess input, and make good decisions, often with incomplete information. While learning new behaviors themselves, deans must also push faculty to demonstrate more initiative and resourcefulness (Barnes, 1996).

An understanding of how community colleges are financed is particularly important in these times of changing philosophies and trends. For a number of years, community colleges could depend on an additional increment of funding each year. State funding formulas were usually based on inputs (such as contact hours, credit hours, full-time equivalent students, or square footage). Although funding based on inputs is still the norm, current trends focus on performance-based funding models. Performance-based funding is not based on inputs; rather, funding is provided based on an achieved level of outcomes. Examples of outcomes used in funding models are number of students who transfer, number of students who graduate, satisfaction level of students or employers (or both), number of credit hours taught by faculty, and attainment of goals set by the institution. Under the input models, the dean's primary responsibility regarding funding was to ensure that the courses were available for increased levels of enrollment. With performance-based models, colleges will be funded for outcomes over which deans have control (at least to the extent that anyone has control over student behavior such as transfer or graduation). It is therefore more important than ever before that deans understand how community colleges operate within their financial contexts.

Roles in Financial Management

The dean, whether he or she is the chief academic officer or reports to the chief academic officer, has a number of roles to play in financial management: developing the budget, managing the budget, brokering resources, and leading program review. In addition, the dean has a role, albeit small at most community colleges, in institutional fundraising.

Budget Development. It is typical for instructional administrators, including the dean, to feel that they have no real impact on the budget or its development. Frequently a copy of the previous year's budget is provided to each department, and budget development consists only of transferring those numbers forward, often with a slight increase across all categories, as the budget request for the coming year. Budget requests are not tied to the institutional plan, and academic departments rarely evaluate their performance for the past year when making the budget request. Under this model it is difficult to find anyone who can explicitly articulate the contribution to the college's mission from these particular expenditures.

Planning and budget development must be linked. In business it has long been understood that the budget is a plan stated in financial terms (Haimann and Hilgert, 1987). Community college deans need to incorporate this thinking as they work with department chairs and faculty to develop program area budgets.

Each department should begin the budget development process with a review of the college's mission, goals, and objectives, not with the current year's budget. These discussions, led by the dean, can begin several months before the finance office distributes budget preparation sheets. Specific action plans should be developed that state how the department will contribute to the achievement of the college's goals and objectives. After working with each department, the dean should align and consolidate the action plans into a broader instructional plan. In a college with several academic deans, this process should be conducted as a group. In this way, resources can be used synergistically. When the finance department begins the annual budget development process, budget requests can then be tied to these action plans. Using such a process ensures that each person in the department participates in budget development and understands the purposes of any allocated resources. In a study of twenty-five community colleges in thirteen states, Halford (1994) reports that one of the principles for raising faculty morale is thorough and open access to budget development. Along with the condition of the physical environment; appropriate participatory management; open communications; honest, even-handed administrators; control over classroom-related matters; adequate instructional support services; opportunities for professional growth; and meaningful involvement in setting and evaluating institutional mission, goals, and objectives, involvement in the budget development process provides the basis for the "reshaping of existing resources for a more effective learning environment" (p. 6). In addition, it gives the dean a level of understanding of program area needs that will be valuable as he or she participates in budget discussions with the wider college community.

A budget developed in such a manner will be much easier to defend during institutional budget hearing processes and will increase the likelihood of receiving the requested allocations. The danger lies with the exposure of pet projects that do not add a great deal of value to the institution. Some of these may have been developed with the minimal use of resources and over the years have developed substantial budgets without scrutiny. A new dean should be cautious when approaching budget development, no matter what method is used. It is imperative to understand the institutional climate and culture when directing how resources will be allocated. What may seem like a project that adds little value may be a tradition that has a firm institutional commitment.

Budget Management. The dean ensures that the allocated budget is managed appropriately. Monitoring the instructional plan is an important part of that process. Other budget management issues are dealing with the finance office and monitoring departmental or program area expenditures.

Often it seems as though the finance office is using its numerous procedures to block the use of resources. It is most important for the dean to learn how the finance office operates and to develop a respectful relationship with its staff. There are many federal, state, and local regulations with which the finance office must comply. When the finance office staff perceive the dean as trying to work with them in promoting the college's mission, they often take steps to assist.

Deans should carefully study and analyze significant variations from the budget to determine why expenditures are not meeting expectations. There is generally opportunity for adjustments throughout the year. These budget revisions should reflect any changes in the department. It is critical that the dean monitor expenditures to ensure that one department does not overextend its budget to the detriment of others. Many faculty and instructional administrators imagine that budgets are imposed to keep resources from them and that the institution has vast hidden resources to bail them out. For most community colleges, this is simply not true. At the beginning of the budget year, the dean should carefully review the budgets under his or her control to ensure that allocations match expectations. Although many colleges still provide documents monthly for a budget status review, the advent of networked computer systems allows on-line budget status review. As this becomes the norm, deans will need to participate in training in the use of the finance system. Without the monthly budget reports as a reminder, they will need to set up their own schedules for budget status review. Monthly is probably too often for a detailed review at the beginning of the fiscal year but not often enough near the end.

It is just as important for the dean to intervene when a department is not spending its budget allocation as it is when a department is overspending. If the plan is to be achieved, each department must do its part; a department that is not spending its allocation may not be implementing its plan. If is it determined that the budget allocated is not needed, the earlier the dean knows this, the sooner the resources can be reallocated to a program where additional funds are needed.

Broker of Resources. The creation of a climate in which student learning is valued is perhaps the most important responsibility of any academic dean. The dean can and should use the resources under his or her control to provide institutional focus on teaching and learning. Resources can be deployed to reward faculty participation in initiatives to assess student learning. And activities that are found to be successful in enhancing student learning can be encouraged and replicated through the judicious use of resources.

As a broker of resources, the dean can invest in making change happen. Some of the ways the dean can accomplish this include release time for faculty, enabling faculty to attend conferences, and encouraging faculty to visit other community colleges.

A study of community college faculty conducted in 1989 found that dissatisfaction with growth opportunities was one of only five satisfaction factors that were found to be significant predictors of a faculty member's intent to leave his or her current position (McBride, Munday, and Tunnell, 1992). Enabling faculty members to attend conferences can be a particularly effective way to ensure that faculty feel satisfied with growth opportunities and to encourage change. Most community colleges have some mechanism to allow faculty to travel for professional development. Deans should be active in this process, identifying conferences that will introduce new ideas and matching appropriate faculty for attendance. Although some faculty resent additional responsibilities, many feel honored to be encouraged to attend a particular conference and take a great deal of responsibility for initiating activities based on the information they gained as a result of that participation. The dean who encourages such activity both contributes to an important satisfaction factor for faculty and facilitates change for the institution.

Visits to other community colleges can be an inexpensive and effective way to invest in facilitating change. Small groups of faculty and instructional administrators frequently can make day trips to nearby colleges where colleagues can exchange ideas. The planning process to make appropriate changes can even begin on the trip home.

Release time, or providing a faculty member with a reduced teaching load, is a time-honored method of supporting individual faculty members as they participate in special projects. Regarding release time, administrators have been heard to moan, "Why do we have to provide incentives just to get faculty to do their jobs?" While release time is sometimes overused, its benefit as a tool to encourage faculty members to spend time in projects the dean deems valuable cannot be overlooked. It is incumbent on the dean to find projects and activities that will accomplish institutional goals and to use resources, including release time, to support them.

Program Review. Program review is an important part of academic economics. In some community colleges, each program is evaluated annually; in others, the program is reviewed on a multiyear cycle. For some, program review is entirely a local matter; for others, the state provides the time line and framework. The focus of program review is often purely economic. However, it should involve other program quality issues as well. Items typically scrutinized include number of credit hours (or contact hours) taught by faculty (full time, part time, and as overload), number of credit hours (or contact hours) generated by students, student head count enrollment, revenue generated, expenses incurred, revenue/cost ratio, unit cost of instruction for program (cost per credit hour), class size, and full-time-equivalent faculty assigned to program. Program review information must be considered longitudinally; one bad semester should not be used to close a program. In addition, deans must be careful of comparisons from program to program, because each will have special considerations. Finally, programs must be evaluated based on their interrelationships. For example, since nursing classes are limited in size by accreditation and state regulations, they are seldom cost-effective. Yet without nursing students, other courses, such as biology, would not have such high enrollments. If a nursing program is closed or curtailed, the impact will ripple throughout the college.

Whatever the program review cycle is, deans will need to make decisions regarding program offerings on a semester (or quarter) basis. The decision to offer certain classes when the class schedule is being developed arises from student need, faculty desire to teach certain courses, and the determination on the part of the instructional administrator that this course will generate enough student enrollments to pay for itself. This break-even analysis for courses and programs information will be used again at the start of the term when the decision is made to cancel classes that do not have sufficient enrollments.

Every dean should know the break-even point for the courses for which he or she is responsible. This number depends on the amount of funding per credit hour (contact hour or full-time equivalents). A course will break even when the revenue (from the various revenue sources) generated by the enrollments in the course equals the direct cost of offering the course (generally the faculty salary). In order for a program or course to be considered cost-effective, it must generate more funding than the break-even amount. Because the break-even formula does not take into account the overhead for courses or programs (for example, instructional support salaries, library, facilities, and instructional equipment), courses should generally enroll substantially more students than the break-even number. Break-even analysis will be moderated by the manner in which funds are received and thus vary from state to state. For example, if a state provides categorical funding for facilities maintenance or libraries, those costs will not need to be covered as a part of overhead. In spite of state funding differences, there are two formulas for assessing program cost-effectiveness that generally work for states with an average mixture of funding:

150–165 percent formula. For a course or program to be cost-effective, it must generate 150 to 165 percent of the cost of salary and fringe benefits in state funding.

65 percent formula. No more than 65 percent of the state money generated by a course should go to pay the salary and fringe benefits of the instructor if the course is to be considered cost-effective.

The ideal faculty-student ratio varies from state to state and from discipline to discipline because states provide reimbursement at different levels and often reimburse each discipline at a different rate. However, an institution-wide average faculty-student ratio of 1:24 is considered ideal for most funding mechanisms; a ratio of 1:20 approaches good academic management. If the ratio is less than 1:20, the funding is probably not sufficient to finance instruction.

Fundraising. Although much has been written recently about the increased role of fundraising in community colleges, little of this addresses the role of the academic dean. The dean is not often involved in the development of fundraising strategy or in the intricacies of making the ask, yet it is essential that the dean understand the college's fundraising plan and contribute to the success of that plan.

Perhaps the most important contribution of the dean is the assurance of the viability and reputation of the academic programs. It is very important to most donors that they are giving to an institution that is highly respected and will be in operation long into the future. For the community college dean, this requires that graduates, who usually remain in the community, are well prepared for their careers and community citizenship. It is essential that program advisory committees play an active role in the development and evaluation of curricula. It is also important that the dean develop connections in the community and invite people who can make a contribution to serve on program advisory committees. Several types of contributions are required, including the ability to engage in meaningful program content discussions, the contribution of resources specifically directed to the program (such as specialized equipment), the ability to hire program graduates, the contribution of resources to the college as a whole, and the ability to make connections with others who can contribute to the program and the college.

At times the dean must become more actively involved in fundraising. The dean may be invited to special events associated with fundraising or be asked to participate in the one-on-one discussions that take place between the potential donor and the development office. In most cases the dean is invited to establish credibility for a program or plan. Prior to attending such a meeting, the dean should find out what his or her role will be and be prepared to provide the appropriate information to support the development office.

What Deans Need to Know

Several topics are fundamental to a CAO's understanding of his college's financial situation.

Categories of Income. A dean needs to become very familiar with the funding mechanisms that support his or her college. In 1973 the Institute of Higher Education at the University of Florida, under the direction of James L. Wattenbarger, began publishing a series of books on the financing of community colleges. Each edition was based on a survey sent to the office responsible for community colleges in each state. In 1988 the American Association of Community Colleges (AACC) undertook responsibility for this series; the most recent report in the series is *Community College Financing 1990: Challenges for a New Decade,* published by AACC in 1991. More recent information on funding trends is available in the *AACC Annual* (most recent is the 1998–1999 edition), which provides an in-depth look at community colleges on a state-by-state basis.

Funding for community colleges comes, in varying degrees, from student tuition and fees and from state, local, and federal sources. In 1988 the average funding by percentage of all funds available was 58.16 percent from the state, 12.93 percent from local sources, 21.67 percent from student tuition and fees, 2.7 percent from the federal government, and 4.23 percent from other sources (Honeyman, Williamson, and Wattenbarger, 1991). By 1995–1996 these percentages were 39 percent from the state, 18 percent from local sources, 20 percent from student tuition and fees, 13 percent from the federal government, and 10 percent from other sources (American Association of Community Colleges, 1998). In general colleges are receiving a lower percentage of operating funds from state sources. Funding provided by the state ranges from nearly 100 percent to less than 25 percent.

State appropriations are made on the basis of program costs for nearly half the states (Honeyman, Williamson, and Wattenbarger, 1991). When program costs are considered, funding is generally provided in differential amounts for credit hours, contact hours, or FTEs (full-time-equivalent students) depending on the program area. It is important for the dean to know how funding is generated and to be aware of the relative amounts that each program area generates. This is important information to use when determining which classes to offer and how many students are required if a class is not to be canceled. Other mechanisms through which state funding is provided include performance funding, workload formulas, expenditure-driven formulas, previous budget plus an inflation factor and adjustments for special projects, allocation for square footage, and funding for various other categorical programs.

Local tax revenue is most often provided through property taxes. Over half of the states report that local taxes are available as a funding source to community colleges (Honeyman, Williamson, and Wattenbarger, 1991).

Student tuition and fees increased an average of nearly 14 percent from 1985 to 1989 (Honeyman, Williamson, and Wattenbarger, 1991). This trend has continued, with public community college average tuition and fees increasing 4.7 percent from 1998–1999 to 1999–2000. This increase well exceeds the 2.3 percent increase in the consumer price index ("Local Community Colleges," 1999).

As state financing for community colleges decreases, the burden of funding is passed on to the students. Additional fees for parking, technology, student activities, materials, and other avenues are becoming a more common funding resource.

Federal government financing for community colleges comes in the form of student financial aid, funding for vocational programs, the Carl D. Perkins Vocational Applied Technology Education Act (VATEA), and special purpose grants, such as from the Fund for the Improvement of Post-Secondary Education, the National Science Foundation, Title III, and Trio. As resources decline, competition for federal grants increases. A number of workshops are available to assist in the preparation of various federal grants. In order to be competitive, it is a good idea to participate in one of these before writing a major grant application.

Other sources of funding include revenues from auxiliary services (such as bookstores), grants from private foundations, and resources from fundraising initiatives. Colleges that are able to take advantage of these specialized funding sources generally have active development offices to assist in the identification and nurturing of these opportunities.

Local Tax Assessment. Local taxes are assessed and collected under the direction of the board of trustees. In order for a board to have the authority to levy taxes or special assessments, it must be established by the vote of the citizens of the district, and board members must be elected according to state law. Taxes levied by local boards are generally ad valorem taxes based on the value of property in the district. There is usually a range within which tax rates can be set without an election. In some cases special assessments, such as for building projects, can also be levied without putting the question to the voters.

Financing New Construction. The options for financing new construction are constrained by state and local laws. Deans should be aware of how new construction is financed and should know what obligations a board is assuming if it is to issue bonds. Revenue bonds are often offered by community colleges to finance construction. The principal and interest for revenue bonds are payable exclusively from pledged revenues. For example, a community college might add a student fee that would then be pledged toward the principal and interest for revenue bonds, the proceeds of which would be used to finance a student activities center.

Some states have a process for applying for state funding for construction. This process generally requires the development of a proposal documenting need, which is reviewed by the state community college office. The project is placed on a statewide list in priority order. Projects are on this list for varying amounts of time depending on state legislative appropriations. Deans who are in the need of additional facilities for programs should investigate this process and work with the financial office to prepare the appropriate documentation.

Key Accounting Terminology. The dean must be familiar with the general operating principles for financial management (these depend on state and local regulations and requirements) and several key concepts. Some important accounting terms are found in the glossary later in this chapter.

Challenges for Deans

Many deans are not prepared for their financial management roles. Research by Townsend and Bassoppo-Moyo (1996) indicates that for academic administrators, competence in budgeting and finance was frequently identified as lacking. To get the formal training they desire, many deans take advantage of the increasing number of graduate programs for community college leadership. These programs should make a community college finance and organization course a required part of the program (Townsend and Bassoppo-Moyo, 1996). At the very least a section of the requisite community college history course should focus on finance issues. In addition, sessions on community college financial management should be included regularly at national conferences aimed at providing professional development for deans and other instructional administrators.

Most deans move from a department or discipline to the position of academic dean. In doing so, it is essential that they shift their focus from that department to a collegewide view. Although this challenge is also felt in areas other than financial management, it is particularly important that the dean acquire a global sense of the college's financial resources quickly if he or she is to be an effective advocate. As a first step, a new dean should request that the chief financial officer spend some time briefing him or her on the institutional budget and various other financial considerations. This could be the same sort of information that the chief financial officer might provide to a new board member as part of that orientation process. The college's strategic planning committee is also a good place for a dean to acquire a global view of the college. And, of course, the dean should review any planning documents, accreditation reports, college histories, and other useful materials.

The rate of change in society and in community colleges is a challenge that is certainly not felt by deans alone. Copa and Ammentorp (1997) write, "As presently organized and delivered, higher education is no longer sustainable, technologically or pedagogically" (p. 1). In a project "to provide a framework through which two-year institutions can move toward new designs" (p. 2), they provide seven new design specifications for the financial management of community colleges. With a value-centered management approach, these new designs call for the focus of "management attention on the outcomes of education" (p. 18), a move that will require more active participation on the part of academic deans in the financial management of community colleges. Their "Design Specifications for Learning Finance" call for an alignment of finances with the learning context; an integration of multiple funding sources for greater flexibility; a linkage of responsibility, performance, and reward; the support of reengineering and innovative actions; the use of partnerships as a standard way of doing business; the allocation of resources based on value added; and the stabilization of funding patterns.

In this changing environment in which costs for higher education increase and traditional sources are providing declining amounts of funding, deans are being asked to provide higher-quality services with flat or reduced budgets. Participation in budget development, encouraging involvement of faculty, a holistic perspective on program review, and involvement in fundraising are essential activities for today's academic deans.

Glossary of Accounting Terms

Some important accounting words to know follow (adapted from Wilson, Hay, and Kattellus, 1998):

Account number. A system of numbering or otherwise designating accounts in such a manner that the symbol used reveals quickly certain required information, e.g., all instructional accounts might begin with the number, "5," all accounts for materials might have a "4" as the second number in the account, etc. In this way expenses can be classified and reports of the amount budgeted or expended for specific classes of items, e.g., travel, can be quickly prepared.

Ad valorem. A basis for levy of taxes upon property based on the value of property "in proportion to its value."

Allocation. A part of an appropriation designated for expenditure by specific organization units and/or for special purposes or activities.

Apportionment. The distribution of an institution's appropriation into amounts available for specified time periods.

Appropriation. An authorization granted by a legislative body to incur liabilities for purposes specified in the appropriation act (the legal action giving the authorization to acquire goods, services, or facilities to be used for purposes specified in the act).

Audit. The examination of financial records and procedures to verify that statements prepared from the accounts present fairly the financial position and results of financial operations in accordance with generally accepted accounting principles and to determine compliance with applicable laws and regulations. Audits may also review the efficiency and economy with which operations were carried out and/or the effectiveness in achieving program results.

Capital outlay. Expenditures which result in the acquisition of or addition to fixed assets (assets of a long-term character which are intended to continue to be held or used, such as land, buildings, machinery, furniture, and other equipment).

Encumbrances. Financial commitments in the form of purchase orders, contracts, or salary commitments for which funds are reserved. They cease to be encumbrances when paid or when the actual liability is recorded.

Pro Forma. This term is used in conjunction with a noun, e.g., pro forma budget, to denote that the contents of the presentation may be either wholly or partially hypothetical, actual facts, estimates, or proposals and are provided for form's sake.

References

American Association of Community Colleges. *AACC Annual, 1998–99.* Washington, D.C.: Community College Press, 1998.

Anderson, W. M. "Characteristics, Preparation, and Attitudes of Selected Public Junior-Community College Deans of Instruction." Unpublished doctoral dissertation, Southern Illinois University at Carbondale, 1973. (ED 100 421)

Barnes, T. "The Chair as Entrepreneurial Leader: How to Increase Support and Funding for Your Department or Area." Paper presented at the Annual International Conference of the National Community College Chair Academy, Phoenix, Ariz., Feb. 14–17, 1996. (ED 394 550)

Cohen, A. M. (ed.). *Perspectives on the Community College: Essays by John Lombardi.* Washington, D.C.: American Association of Community and Junior Colleges and the American Council on Education, 1992.

Copa, G. H., and Ammentorp, W. *New Designs for the Two-Year Institution of Higher Edu-*

cation. Berkeley: University of California-Berkeley, National Center for Research in Vocational Education, 1997.

Haimann, T., and Hilgert, R. L. *Supervision: Concepts and Practices of Management.* (4th ed.) Cincinnati, Ohio: South-Western, 1987.

Halford, A. "Faculty Morale—Enhancing It in Spite of Diminishing Resources and Challenges." Paper presented at the International Conference for Community College Chairs, Deans, and Other Instructional Leaders, Phoenix, Ariz., Feb. 23–26, 1994. (ED 368 422)

Honeyman, D., Williamson, M. L., and Wattenbarger, J. *Community College Financing 1990: Challenges for a New Decade.* Washington, D.C.: American Association of Community and Junior Colleges, 1991.

"Local Community Colleges a 'Great Value.'" *Community College Times,* 1999, *11,* 1.

McBride, S. A., Munday, R. G., and Tunnell, J. "Community College Faculty Job Satisfaction and Propensity to Leave." *Community/Junior College Quarterly of Research and Practice,* 1992, *16,* 157–165.

Townsend, B., and Bassoppo-Moyo, S. "If I'd Only Known: Administrative Preparation That Could Have Made a Difference." Paper presented at the Annual Meeting of the American Educational Research Association, New York, Apr. 8–12, 1996. (ED 396 641)

Wilson, E. R., Hay, L. E., and Kattellus, S. *Accounting for Governmental and Nonprofit Entities.* (11th ed.) Burr Ridge, Ill.: Irwin, 1998.

SUSAN A. MCBRIDE is president at Jefferson Davis Community College in Brewton, Alabama. She formerly served as academic vice president at Black Hawk College in Moline, Illinois, and at Northeast Texas Community College in Mt. Pleasant, Texas. She has been active in the National Council of Instructional Administrators for some time and sits on the national board.

8

What is the difference between information and data?
Understanding how information can be alchemized into
useful data is a key to survival in the Information Age.

Community College Alchemists:
Turning Data into Information

George H. Johnston and Sharon A. R. Kristovich

> Why can't we get the data we want?
> > Senior administrator (before institutional research)

> The institutional research staff has been able to conceptualize
> data collection strategies and communicate understanding and
> support throughout the process. That's really thinking outside the
> box.
> > Dean of continuing education (after institutional research)

Does either of these statements sound familiar? If your college responds as
the dean of continuing education did, you probably do not need to read this
chapter. However, if your college continues to be faced with the problem of
too much data and not enough information, read on. This chapter examines
how one community college has developed a national Bellwether
Award–winning data-driven decision-making process that uses its institutional research (IR) staff to make the transition from data to information.

Dennis Jones of the National Center for Higher Education Management
Systems (NCHEMS) has suggested that one reason that institutions may
have difficulty turning data into information may lie in the failure to understand the basic distinctions between them (Jones, 1998). A datum is an
item's measurement; information is a user-directed presentation of that measurement. What administrators often think is "data" is actually "information," and an appropriate facility is needed to provide the transformation.

The institutional research office is often designated to be responsible
for keeping data and transforming those data into information. According

to McLaughlin, Howard, Balkan, and Blythe (1998), institutional researchers play three key roles in providing the support necessary to transform data into information: as custodian or keeper of the data, as broker of the process of transferring the data into information, and as manager or processor of the information and application to a situation. To perform these roles, the institutional researcher must have knowledge of the data and how to obtain them, their proposed use, and ways to turn them into the desired information.

The academic manager, whether a department dean or chief academic officer (CAO), is among the primary consumers of institutional data. Chairs "generally assume the role of doing whatever is necessary to fulfill departmental and campus goals and are crucial to the success and survival of an institution" (Kranitz and Patterson, 1996, p. 438). The institutional researcher therefore has the responsibility to make a variety of information available to meet the academic managers' needs in a timely fashion. Institutional researchers are also charged with educating deans and the CAO about the properties of the information they are receiving. Therefore, academic managers and institutional researchers need to work closely together and communicate their information needs clearly.

This chapter characterizes some of the data and resulting information that Parkland College's Institutional Research Office has produced that might be useful to department chairs. In these characterizations, we identify issues and concerns that this information has produced.

Data and Information Defined

Data and information have different properties. According to Jones (1998), data have certain characteristics, or properties, and these properties are associated with measurement and are essentially technical issues—for example:

Validity, the extent to which the measure actually represents the intended construct
Reliability, or the extent the measure will be the same if repeated
Accuracy, or how close the measurement comes to being error free

If the data are perceived to be inaccurate or unreliable, then they have little or no value to decision makers. However, being able to provide accurate, reliable data is not sufficient for making good data-driven decisions. The decision-making process must also take into consideration the properties of information, which are associated with users, uses, and the context of use:

Relevance, or whether the information reduces the uncertainty associated with a specific use or decision
Acceptability, or the extent to which the message can be heard by the user
Timeliness, or the availability when needed

Integrity, or the extent the information is derived from accurate sources, preserved in the analytical process, and correctly translated by the "receiver" as intended by the "sender"

The Institutional Research Office at Parkland uses data and information properties to fill requests of middle management (deans, directors, and department chairs). To ensure acceptability and integrity, an explanation of the situational caveats is provided in information requests. As a result, middle management is better able to integrate information into the decision-making process. If the following quotations are indicative, then Parkland's Institutional Research Office has been instrumental in helping community college middle management improve their decision-making process. According to the humanities department chair, "Institutional research has responded promptly to every request for information (and it has received MANY requests). The information was explained to me in such a way that I can help instructors understand their own results in context, thereby helping them to interpret their results" (K. Keener, personal communication, Aug. 18, 1999). The mathematics department chair put it this way: "The data IR have helped to generate on trends of grades of students tracking through our algebra sequence has helped shed light on issues we knew were lurking somewhere there in the shadows. Now we see some of the problems, we can debate the issues and make some changes to try to improve the situation" (J. Hall, personal communication, Aug. 19, 1999).

Data Warehouse Management

The process of collecting good data in order to be able to turn them into information begins with collecting and storing the data in ways that ensure quick and easy retrieval. This function is sometimes referred to as data warehouse management. Probably the most important source of data is the student registration database, but there are several problems with using the database directly. One is that the contents of the database are constantly changing, and consistency of the data is a critical component of accuracy and reliability. If there are 8,431 students reported one day and 8,612 on another report using data taken several weeks later, credibility is significantly undermined. Second, data must be quickly available. Under the old system at Parkland, where all data resided on the mainframe, the Institutional Research Office had to compete with student registration and payroll for use of the mainframe. Obviously others had higher priority; but when the president is about to meet with a local high school superintendent and wants to know how many students from that system are currently enrolled, she does not want to hear that she must wait two or three hours. Parkland's solution was to migrate the data from the mainframe to a PC-based system that uses SPSS, a statistical analysis software application (Kristovich and Johnston, 1998a).

Parkland made the decision to mirror mainframe data on a PC database by creating a snapshot of the registration data and placing it into an SPSS data set. The snapshot process involves identifying and capturing a core set of registration variables at various times in the semester. Data from the current semester are collected at key times (for example, the tenth day and fifth week). Data from past semesters are captured at the end of the term and thus do not reflect the changes that often occur throughout the semester. This core set of variables was developed through discussions with department chairs and senior administrators, so that a comprehensive and relatively static variable list could be developed. The creation of the PC-based mirror of the mainframe eliminated the problem of resource sharing, and information is provided in a timely manner. There is limited access to the PC database, so the demand on the server is minimal, and requests for information can be filled quickly. Also, because the same definitions are used to capture the data and only one time interval per term is selected, the reliability and accuracy of the information provided to users were significantly improved.

The PC database is now the primary source for research data at Parkland. Requests for information have increased exponentially since it became operational in late FY '97. The database is used to produce a variety of information such as college fact books, enrollment management, program review, graduate follow-up reports, and other reports that can be used by department chairs and administrators in decision-making. The remaining sections discuss these pieces of information and their uses for department chairs and administrators.

College Fact Books

One of the uses of the PC database is to generate data to create fact books. The fundamental purpose of a fact book is to provide documented information about the institution for decision making, rather than relying on personal memory, anecdote, or bias. "Knowing the score is better than flying by the seat of your pants" (Marks, 1996, p. 27). Fact books contain information, which is derived from data sources such as the PC database. In the transformation from data to information, the data must be presented in such a way that the user can understand the original intent (Jones, 1998). Because there are numerous decisions or intents at an institution, it should come as no surprise that fact books come in various forms to address the needs of various constituencies.

Parkland College uses two different fact books, which vary in scope and format, for different audiences. The first, which the college refers to as the *Environmental Scanning Data,* is available as a brochure or on the Internet (http://www.parkland.cc.il.us/oire/envirn.htm). This fact book is designed for the general college audience; copies are distributed to the general public as well as to individuals at planning conferences, collegewide discus-

Table 8.1. Parkland Employee Groups by Employment Status

	Full Time	Part Time	Total
Total employees, October 1, 1998	381	371	752
Administrators	30	0	30
Faculty	146	292	438
Confidential staff	12	0	12
Public safety	9	0	9
Support professional staff	81	12	93
Non-academic staff	103	14	117
Other part time	53	0	53
Total faculty, October 1, 1998	146	292	438
Asian American	3	9	12
Native American	1	0	1
Black, Non-Hispanic	6	12	18
Hispanic	N/A	3	3
International	1	3	4
White, Non-Hispanic	136	260	396
Women	69	148	217
Men	77	144	221
Faculty load, fall 1998	53.5%	46.5%	100%

Source: Kristovich and Johnston (1998b, p. 3).

sions, and leadership training. The *Environmental Scanning* document, updated annually at the end of the fall semester, provides information that answers nineteen of the most frequently asked questions about the college, such as, "Who are our credit students?" "What is our enrollment?" and "Who are Parkland graduates?" The information is presented in the form of summary tables, with no narrative, which allows the users to draw their own conclusions. The data sources for this fact book are numerous and include the PC database, the Graduate Follow-up Study, student satisfaction surveys, admissions data, annual employee snapshot, college budget, college catalog, census data, and county unemployment statistics.

Table 8.1 gives an example of the information that is presented to address the question, "Who are Parkland's employees?" The information presented in Table 8.1 was obtained from an annual snapshot taken on the first day of October of every year. Since the number and percentage of part-time staff varies from semester to semester, a common snapshot date allows for annual data comparisons.

The second form of fact book, referred to as *Performance Indicators*, is designed primarily for middle and upper management decision makers and comes in two versions. The much longer version is used by senior administration and the shared governance collegewide planning committee (which includes a representative from the academic department chairs). The shorter version is made available to all members of the campus community. The *Performance Indicators* fact book consists of eight major sections, each with a number of indicators containing one or more sets of information obtained from a variety of sources. The major sections of the *Performance Indicators* document are listed below with the number of indicators listed in parentheses:

Maintenance of Institution's Assets—5-Year Trends (four)
Budget Flexibility (four)
Enrollment Patterns—5-Year Trends (four)
Student Achievement (six)
Participation and Service to Region (four)
Diversity (ten)
Utilization of Assets—5-Year Trend Data (ten)
Economic Accessibility/Affordability (four)
Client Service and Satisfaction (three)

Some of the indicators contain benchmarks where those marks have been established. Three formats are used to facilitate the presentation of the information to the user: graphs, tables, and a brief narrative. *Performance Indicators* provides more interpretation of the information than does *Environmental Scanning Data*, but all the information is offered in a format to encourage users to draw their own conclusions. The following summary contains professional development information, an indicator in the "Maintenance of Institution's Assets" section:

> Our principle is people. "People assets" also need maintenance called professional development. The targeted goal for the ratio of professional development expenditures with respect to salaries and benefits is 2%–5% (NCHEMS). The 5-year trend data indicates there is a yearly average *increase* in spending on professional development of 7.8%. FY 98 (the most recent year for which data are available) shows that a total of $715,738 was spent on all categories of professional development. This represents approximately 3.1% of the annual expenditures on salaries and benefits—well within the range suggested by NCHEMS. The 5-year trend data for the ratio of professional development to salaries and benefits is 3.0%.

The second version of the *Performance Indicators* document is shorter so that it can be more easily distributed to the campus community. This document contains fifteen of the most critical indicators from the first version, along with supporting information. The supporting information is presented in a narrative only; no tables or figures are included.

Fact books provide a convenient, quick reference to general college information for academic managers. Most general questions about the college can often be addressed with either the *Environmental Scanning Data* or *Performance Indicators,* eliminating redundant information requests, improving departmental autonomy, and encouraging critical thinking about the college by all campus units.

Institutional Self-Study

Another area in which information provided by the Institutional Research Office can facilitate administrators' decision making is with the institutional self-study. The institutional self-study often corresponds to the college's regional accreditation and documents the efforts to monitor the campus academic environment, a large undertaking that often involves an analysis of a large variety of information such as the campus climate, student satisfaction, institutional effectiveness, and academic assessment. Parkland's Institutional Research Office has made information and resources available to department chairs and administrators to streamline the self-study process.

In the highly diverse atmosphere of the community, monitoring the campus climate has become a critical component of the institutional self-study process. The use of the term *climate* here is intentional. According to Somers and others (1998), "In the changing campus climate, faculty and staff members are like weather radar. They see the storm clouds approaching and must prepare for the maelstrom of public accountability, the monsoon of post-tenure review, the tornado of diversity, the typhoon of underprepared students, and the thunderstorm of financial difficulties" (p. 35). Hurtado, Carter, and Kardia (1998) use less dramatic images to argue for climate studies of students, but illustrate the importance and the challenge of the campus climate analysis in institutional-self study: "Recently, many campuses have engaged in self-study in order to understand the climate experienced by an increasingly diverse student body. Increases in diverse groups of students have led to both conflict and new campus opportunities for students to learn how to live and work in a complex, diverse society" (p. 53). It is essential for an institution to have a sense of the campus climate to serve its students better (Saunders and Bauer, 1998).

The Institutional Research Office can relieve many of the information headaches associated with the self-study process. The information provided comes in both standard, collegewide survey administration and customized analysis to address more specific research questions. The advantages of both types of information are clear: collegewide assessments such as survey instruments allow for the sharing of information across departments and the observation of interactions among units. Furthermore, these collegewide assessments reduce redundancy of effort and allow for trend analysis. These assessments then free resources for the more detailed analysis needed to improve the quality of education.

Surveys. To understand the campus climate better, Parkland has charged the Office of Institutional Research and Evaluation with developing, administering, and analyzing two biennial student surveys. The *Student Satisfaction Survey*, first administered in the fall 1995 semester and again in the fall 1997 semester, was designed to assess students' satisfaction with a number of student programs and services. A sample of nearly two thousand students from selected courses (approximately one-quarter of the credit students enrolled) participated in each administration. The results from this study were used by administrators to meet one of their institutional effectiveness requirements for regional accreditation.

In addition to questions on student programs and services in the *Student Satisfaction Survey*, students were asked to respond to a series of questions designed to measure their experiences with discrimination both in and out of the classroom. Nearly 92 percent of the students reported "Never" or "Seldom" experiencing discrimination in the classroom. Although this is good news, administrators must take care when interpreting these results. Here, additional sources of information will increase the validity of the data and the integrity of the information.

Partly as a result of the need to develop a shorter form of the *Student Satisfaction Survey* and partly to improve the integrity of the discrimination information, a second biennial student survey was constructed to address how students perceived the diversity climate at the college. The second student survey, the *Diversity Climate Survey*, was created and administered in the spring 1999 semester. It is anticipated that the *Diversity Climate Survey* will be repeated in alternate years with the *Student Satisfaction Survey*. This survey was constructed after models of existing climate surveys. A sample of nearly eighteen hundred students from selected courses (approximately one-quarter of the credit students enrolled) participated in the study. The purpose of the survey was to highlight diversity issues such as discrimination, class content, faculty and student composition, and social interactions along various lines: gender, race and ethnicity, sexual orientation, disability status, and religion. Demographic data such as gender, ethnicity, age, sexual orientation, disability status, and major were also gathered. Students were given the option to comment on any experiences they have had at the college that might be appropriate to the study.

Respondents were asked to indicate how important a given statement was, as well as the extent to which they agreed or disagreed with the statement. For example, one of the statements is, "There are good interactions between minority and non-minority racial students in classes." The students were asked to indicate the level of importance with a three-point scale and agreement or no experience with the statement with a five-point scale. The survey contained sixty-nine questions, many with the dual importance and agreement scales. The underlying research question sought to determine if there was evidence to suggest that attitudes on climate contributed to a stated intent to return or not return the following semester.

Campus climate is not limited to the measurement of student attitudes and satisfaction, but also examines the satisfaction and attitudes of the faculty, staff, and administration. As part of Parkland's continuous efforts to characterize the campus climate, employee parallels to the *Student Satisfaction* and *Diversity Climate* surveys are being developed. These measures are expected to benefit department chairs and administrators by providing useful feedback on the culture in their unit.

Customized Analysis. In addition to the information provided by scheduled satisfaction and climate assessments, the Institutional Research Office is often called on to provide customized research support for a unit's self-study. One of the most important (and difficult) areas of support provided to academic managers in institutional self-study has been in the area of academic outcomes assessment, an item of particular importance to the regional accreditation process. Here, the Institutional Research Office addresses each department's need separately, providing customized solutions for various information needs.

One example of a customized analysis was tracking the sequence that students tended to follow when completing their general education courses. It came as little surprise that students tended to take their composition requirements in or shortly after the first semester in which they were enrolled (in the case of students who "assessed into" developmental English, they started the sequence early in their college experience). An unexpected finding was that students put off fine arts electives until late in their programs. The fine and applied arts department used this finding to develop a new set of courses designed with newer students in mind.

Another example of customized analysis was an attempt to assess written communications across the curriculum. An assessment of writing mechanics was conducted on a stratified sample of students who were taking courses in the general education sequence. Students in identified classes were asked to participate in the study by allowing class-assigned papers to be copied and assessed by an external professional proofreader using a rubric designed by the academic assessment committee. The results showed no significant link between writing mechanics ability and the number of courses that the student had completed. Additional analysis indicated that grade point average (GPA) alone was a significant predictor of success on the writing mechanics assessment. Basically, students who were competent writers when they entered the college remained competent, and students who initially did not know writing mechanics did not learn them while in college. Although these results were somewhat disappointing, the English department used the information obtained from the study as justification for the development of a new course that focused on writing mechanics. The study also demonstrates that departments were willing to share information across departmental lines and that some college-wide assessment of general education objectives was possible.

Enrollment Management

When the Parkland Board of Trustees identified enrollment growth as one of four important goals for the college, the president appointed a special enrollment management team composed of department chairs, the student services director, faculty, and other key staff to develop a plan to increase the enrollment. The Office of Institutional Research, asked to create a method for determining if the team's efforts were making a difference, developed a five-column flowchart developed to track activities and the corresponding results. The flowchart followed a continuous improvement model with a specific goal on the farthest left column, related activities associated with that goal in the second column, and the person responsible for each activity and the status of the activity in the third column. The last two columns were reserved for the results and follow-up activities.

The enrollment management team identified forty-six specific goals, each phrased in such a way that the data collection method was agreed on before the process began. For instance, one goal was to increase collegewide course retention rates by 1 percent. Retention was defined in this case as fewer failing (F) and withdraw (W) grades. Initially there was an increase rather than decrease in the number of F and W grades. As a result, a decision was made to create an additional roster to be completed by faculty during the fifth week of classes. This roster was designed to identify students who could benefit from early interventions by faculty and student support staff (Ayers, Harris, and Johnston, 1999).

Staff on all administrative levels have been highly receptive to this method of tracking the implementation of the enrollment management plan, with the enrollment management team reporting that they are quite pleased with being able to have clear targets. The director of student life wrote, "I have felt that IR has been extremely helpful in areas where there is an inevitable tendency to speculate on trends. Frankly, the ability to ask questions and obtain good data from IR causes me to consistently rethink my perspective on student related issues like retention" (T. Caulfield, personal communication, August 19, 1999). Individual department chairs are satisfied because they participated in setting the goals for their department, as well as being responsible for the activities to achieve the goals. The president is pleased that there is an unambiguous method for determining if the goals are being met. Finally, the board of trustees is pleased because overall enrollments have increased by approximately 2 percent since the plan was implemented. There are probably many explanations for the rising enrollment, and it is not possible to isolate any one set of activities; nevertheless, there is a sense that developing the criteria and data collection methods before implementing the activities has improved the overall decision-making process.

Conclusion

In institutional research, the alchemist's trick of turning lead into gold translates to turning data into information so that administration may make good, sound decisions. The quality of the decisions based on anecdote rather than on solid data is limited. Systems must be put in place that allow the plethora of data to be stored, retrieved, analyzed, and interpreted in a timely and useful manner. An institutional research office is an appropriate place for such data and information to be organized and managed. It can provide a centralized location for maintaining necessary management tools such as fact books, performance indicator documents, customer satisfaction measures, and enrollment management planning. Skilled professional researchers can give a critical advantage to any administrator interested in improving performance.

References

Ayers, J., Harris, Z., and Johnston, G. H. "The Role of the Trustee in Enrollment Management Planning." Paper presented at the annual meeting of the Association of Community College Trustees in Atlanta, Ga., Oct. 13–16, 1999.

Henry, M., and Johnston, G. H. *An Enrollment Management Plan for Parkland College.* Champaign, Ill.: Parkland College, 1999.

Hurtado, S., Carter, D. F., and Kardia, D. "The Climate for Diversity: Key Issues for Institutional Self-Study." In K. W. Baurer (ed.), *Campus Climate: Understanding the Critical Components of Today's Colleges and Universities.* New Directions for Institutional Research, no. 98. San Francisco: Jossey-Bass, 1998.

Jones, D. P. *Data and Information for Executive Decisions in Higher Education.* Denver: National Center for Higher Education Management Systems, 1982.

Jones, D. P. *NCHEMS Data Management Seminar Manual.* Denver: National Center for Higher Education Management Systems, 1998.

Kranitz, G., and Patterson, W. "So You Are a New Chair or Dean: How Do You Perform Your Complex Roles Without Any Formal Training?" Paper presented at the Fifth Annual International Conference Community and Technical College Chairs, Deans, and Other Organizational Leaders, Phoenix/Mesa, Ariz., Feb. 14–17, 1996.

Kristovich, S.A.R., and Johnston, G. H. "Creating an Extraction Database for Student Enrollment Data." Paper presented at the 28th annual meeting of the Illinois Association for Institutional Research, Nov. 1998a.

Kristovich, S.A.R., and Johnston, G. H. *Environmental Scanning Data.* Champaign, Ill.: Parkland College, 1998b.

Kristovich, S.A.R., and Johnston, G. H. "It's Not the Heat, It's the Humidity: Results of a Student Climate Survey at Parkland." Paper presented at the annual meeting of the Illinois Association of Institutional Research, Starved Rock, Ill., Nov. 4–5, 1999.

Marks, J. L. "Toward a New Breed of Fact Book." In L. G. Jones (ed.), *Campus Fact Books: Keeping Pace with New Institutional Needs and Challenges.* New Directions for Institutional Research, no. 91. San Francisco: Jossey-Bass, 1996.

McLaughlin, G. W., Howard, R. D., Balkan, L. A., and Blythe, E. W. *People, Processes, and Managing Data.* Tallahassee, Fla.: Association for Institutional Research, 1998.

Saunders, L. E., and Bauer, K. W. "Undergraduate Students Today: Who Are They?" New Directions for Institutional Research, no. 98. San Francisco: Jossey-Bass, 1998.

Somers, P., and others. "Faculty and Staff: The Weather Radar of Campus Climate." In K. W. Baurer (ed.), *Campus Climate: Understanding the Critical Components of Today's Colleges and Universities.* New Directions for Institutional Research, no. 98. San Francisco: Jossey-Bass, 1998.

GEORGE H. JOHNSTON *is the director of the Office for Institutional Research and Evaluation at Parkland College, Champaign, Illinois.*

SHARON A. R. KRISTOVICH *is research analyst at the Office for Institutional Research and Evaluation at Parkland College, Champaign, Illinois.*

9

As agents of change, deans should be prepared to continue their education by acquiring the vital leadership skills they need through professional development programs.

Preparing Community College Deans to Lead Change

Debra D. Bragg

The position of dean in the community college has a long history and an important future. The most vital functions—transfer, career preparation, community education, and support services—revolve around these administrative leaders who are the linchpins of community college life. Deans create the stage for future operations while managing day-to-day activities. They influence most change in community colleges, and their ideas and behaviors can have a dramatic impact. Ever more diverse in gender and race and ethnicity (Harris and Nettles, 1996), community college leaders can create opportunities for faculty, staff, and students to learn and grow. Although subject matter expertise is important, deans should possess democratic leadership, creative management, and finely tuned human relation skills. To ensure their success, careful attention should be paid to the initial preparation and ongoing professional development of community college deans. Professional development needs to be timely but also continuous, and practical but tied to bold new ideas that do not neglect time-tested theories of the past. Six knowledge areas are central to the creation of a comprehensive professional development system for community college deans.

The Dean's Imperative to Lead Change

Leading change is at the heart of a dean's work. As we begin a new century, we enter a period of transition and renewal in all aspects of the current and future work of the community college. Change is occurring in the people who are employed and who enroll in these institutions: faculty, staff, and students (Phillippe, 1997). Change is apparent in the new shapes and structures assumed by community colleges as organizations and the new governance and inclusive management philosophies being employed there (Gibson-Benninger, Ratcliff, and Rhoads, 1996). Change is also evident in instruction and support services, including more emphasis on learner-centered approaches (O'Banion, 1997), closer alignment of the academic and social functions (Tinto and Russo, 1994), and more enhanced integration of subject matter within the curriculum (Illinois Task Force of Integration, 1997). Stronger relationships are being nurtured through partnerships between community colleges and schools, businesses, and community agencies (Grubb and others, 1997). More attention is being paid to accountability, partly out of necessity (Messick, 1999), but also because of greater recognition of the need to serve an increasingly diverse public. Demonstrating effective performance and positive outcomes for all learners is important to the future of community colleges.

Past writings about professional development for community college leaders have acknowledged the importance of preparing administrators to make sound decisions and manage effectively (see, for example, Cohen and others, 1994). However, often these discussions have focused more on current demands than future opportunities. With so many forces influencing community colleges to be different from the past and better serve new constituents in the future, it is crucial that professional development focus on leadership for change. No doubt concerns about planning, budgeting, personnel management, and the like will always be needed, but new areas of expertise need to be developed to serve a growing diversity of peoples, perspectives, and priorities better. Careful blending of knowledge from the past, present, and future is advantageous to any professional development program.

Essential Knowledge for Community College Deans

To prepare community college deans for leadership, six core knowledge areas are crucial:

- Mission, philosophy, and history
- Learner-centered orientation
- Instructional leadership
- Information and educational technologies
- Institutional accountability and learner assessment
- Administrative preparation

These core areas have emerged through various research activities that my colleagues and I at the University of Illinois at Urbana-Champaign have employed as we seek to expand and strengthen our Community College Leadership graduate program. Consistent with the notion of leadership for change, we believe these areas that we propose are conducive to the creation of a worthwhile graduate program for personnel at any level, and particularly for community college deans.

Mission, Philosophy, and History. Understanding community college mission and philosophy from a historic perspective is of critical importance to the preparation and continued development of deans. Knowing how community colleges emerged, grew, and changed over the twentieth century is highly informative. In an informal poll, Hankin (1996) found consensus among practitioners themselves around the idea of educating leaders about philosophies and missions that have guided the evolution of community colleges. He confirmed that practitioners appreciate having the opportunity to reflect on the past while considering alternative futures. Hankin remarked, "Community college educators are concerned that if they cannot state or describe the functions and missions of their institutions, they will be unable to inform external publics of what the community college contributes. Continual reflection on what we do and why we do it would seem highly appropriate" (p. 39). Amey and Twombly (1992) remind us, however, that much of the written history of community colleges neglects the voices of women and minorities. They challenge community college scholars and practitioners "to create alternative construction(s) of leadership that reflect and convey the rich tradition, history, and spirit of the [entire] community college movement" (p. 147).

Without knowing the history of community colleges, deans have little appreciation for the tremendous growth and importance of these institutions today. Having come from near obscurity in the early twentieth century, community colleges now play a vital role in American higher education. Dougherty has observed, "The community college today is the single largest and most important portal into higher education" (1998, p. 1). Public community colleges enroll 52 percent of all undergraduates, making them the largest single group of higher education students (Phillippe, 1997, p. 20). With such impressive figures, it is possible to get caught up in recruitment exercises to keep numbers high rather than think deeply about the unique characteristics and needs of individual learners who are attending already (Cohen and others, 1994). More important than enrollment management, deans need to understand who their students are and why they are enrolling. Understanding today's students is easier when one has studied the students of the past. By knowing where the institution has been, deans can respond more appropriately to the unique needs of learners of today and tomorrow.

Learning-Centered Orientation. Community college students are a highly diverse group. Although a sizable proportion of students go to community colleges directly after high school, many delay enrollment. Nationally, the average age of community college students is twenty-nine (Phillippe, 1997). Females outnumber males at the two-year level by a ratio of nearly 1.4 to 1. Minority enrollments are also higher in two- than in four-year colleges. Nationally, 56 percent of Hispanic and 51 percent of African American students who attend public colleges and universities enroll in community colleges, compared to 37 percent for white students (Rendon and Garza, 1996). A lack of academic preparedness is also evident in more students who are entering community colleges. Understanding changing student characteristics and determining their impact on teaching and learning is crucial to a dean's job and central to any professional development initiatives designed to meet their needs.

Regardless of their differences in age, race or ethnic affiliation, or academic preparedness, most students have a common goal to pursue a community college education to fulfill practical, employment-related needs. Kantor (1997) argues that all learning in the community college should be linked to career preparation, and she contends that all learner goals can be associated with this perspective. Her depiction of community college learners reveals four categories: the emerging workforce learner, the existing workforce learner, the transitional workforce learner, and the entrepreneurial workforce learner. No doubt Kantor's ideas are controversial, but she reminds us of the importance of knowing a great deal about students. Helping deans think strategically about what students hope to accomplish and how to structure curriculum to maximize their goals is important. Kantor argues, "Education in 15 weeks or in two-year packages may not work. Not only may time frames need to be refashioned but also course content. In this arena of education and training, choices about 'need-to-know' and 'nice-to-know' content have to be made, especially when time and money are limited. For administrators and faculty, responding to these requirements poses learning opportunities as well, i.e., learning through making changes that enhance flexibility and customer focus" (p. 28).

Deans need to be able to assist faculty and staff to serve students through an array of instructional delivery options. Some deans see that their student clientele is changing but do not know how to respond. Their knowledge of how to transform their colleges into more receptive, learner-centered organizations is limited. Rarely do professional development activities delve into the particular characteristics and concerns of learners and the specific approaches that could meet their needs, but they should. More emphasis should be placed on understanding the reciprocal relationship between learners and all facets of the community college enterprise.

Instructional Leadership. Unlike four-year colleges and universities that emphasize a tripartite mission of teaching, research, and service, community colleges focus almost exclusively on teaching as a predominant goal. Leaders of the community college movement have proclaimed community colleges as teaching colleges, attempting to avoid the sharp criticism launched at other higher education institutions for maximizing research at the expense of good teaching. Yet recently community colleges have drawn their own share of criticism. Questions about the quality of teaching coupled with the quality of learning have been raised, partly because of concerns about student retention and academic performance (Grubb, 1999). Such concerns have influenced some experts to argue for placing learning rather than teaching at center stage, as though these functions are unrelated. Have we really only discovered the importance of learning in the past few years? Surely community college educators have valued teaching and learning throughout the history of these institutions. Still, the fundamental questions are important. O'Banion (1997), Cross (1998), and others argue for placing more emphasis on what learners experience and how they benefit. At all levels, administrators (especially deans), faculty, staff, and students are asking themselves what constitutes good teaching and how teaching produces active learning. Ultimately community college personnel are considering how their work contributes to the end goal of learner success.

Advocating the notion of community colleges as "learning colleges," O'Banion (1997) postulates that learning would be enhanced if students became full partners in the learning process. He recommends that students have the primary responsibility for choosing from a wide variety of learning options. According to O'Banion, if collaborative learning were more prevalent, faculty were defined as learning facilitators, and learning outcomes were documented more fully, teaching and learning would be more engaging and effective. To achieve these goals, O'Banion contends that community colleges should move more aggressively to adopt new instructional practices. New resources in time, funding, and supervision are needed to assist faculty in incorporating more constructivist, integrated, and learner-centered approaches, including learning styles, multiple intelligences, and brain-based research. To change teaching and learning dramatically, community college deans need to understand the options and support faculty, staff, and students who engage in the instructional reform process.

Information and Educational Technologies. Community colleges have emphasized the use of technologies from the 1960s onward. Technology has been important for instructional purposes because community colleges, which are predominantly commuter institutions, have had to attend to the needs of students who spend limited time on campus. Educational technologies have emphasized individualized learning, making their application in community colleges a logical step. Closed- and open-circuit television has a lengthy history, going back to the 1950s in the City Colleges of Chicago (Cohen and Brawer, 1996). The 1960s and 1970s saw increasing use of learning laboratories, where self-based instruction was emphasized, using audio and video media. In the 1980s, community colleges began to incorporate personal computers into instructional practices. By 1990, computer labs were commonplace.

A national survey concerning computer usage reported, "Community colleges lead in the percentage of courses reporting classroom computer technology usage, and they use computer-based labs or classrooms in nearly twice as many courses as public university courses" (cited in Cohen and Brawer, 1996, p. 168). Computer-assisted instruction (CAI) for tutorial presentations has become common. Computer-based simulations and more interactive CAI applications are evident today, including assessments to meet individual student needs. Also in the 1990s, distance learning supported by educational technologies and the Internet made dramatic inroads. Use of computer technologies is apparent in other aspects of administration as well, particularly in planning, financial management, supervision, and marketing. Everyday communication over the Internet and e-mail is pervasive, but its adoption is relatively recent in many community colleges. As the future unfolds, changes are sure to happen even more rapidly. Internet and telecommunications networks linking community colleges with K–12 education, four-year colleges and universities, businesses, and government agencies will enhance institutional capabilities. As opportunities arise, community college leaders must keep pace.

Of all personnel, community college deans are probably most in need of information about how technological innovations can be used to achieve institutional, curricular, and program goals. They need to understand the trade-offs in quality, access, and opportunity that are afforded faculty and students when distance versus classroom learning strategies are employed. To make these choices wisely, professional development needs to give deans hands-on knowledge and skills, along with straight talk about the real cost of maintenance and upgrades. Site visits to observe existing applications can help deans better understand the potential impact of new technologies on their own institutions, both positive and negative (Layton, 1996). Armed with up-to-date knowledge, deans can educate their own faculty and staff about the key features of new technologies and how they can be used effectively.

Institutional Accountability and Learner Assessment. Tremendous change has occurred in the area of assessment of institutional, program, and individual outcomes. Prompted by external forces such as changes in accreditation and new governmental emphases on acountability, many community colleges and state community college systems have made concerted efforts to enhance outcomes assessments. Twenty-two states, including several with large community college systems (including California, Illinois, Texas, and Florida), have initiated performance-based funding based on various outcome measures ("9 Issues," 1999). In addition, some community colleges guarantee that their graduates will transfer to four-year colleges and universities or succeed on the job (Bragg and Colwell, 1996). Further, many community colleges invest in Continuous Quality Improvement strategies to link local enhancements to local plans and budgets (O'Banion, 1997). In the future, even more decisions are likely to be linked to performance across all segments of the educational system, K–16 level. To be effective, deans need to understand how their institutions are affected by fiscal decisions, particularly performance-based funding. They should take a more active role in the policymaking process, and professional development activities should prepare them to do so.

In addition to external forces, learner assessment policies and practices are changing within institutions, due partly to changing student demographics and new instructional and technological innovations. As student needs become more diverse and instructional approaches change to accommodate greater diversity, assessments should change too. Deans should understand these developments and incorporate them into their future plans. As instructional leaders, they need to understand the contemporary view that assessment is a vital part of the overall teaching and learning process, not separate from it. Deans can prepare faculty and staff to implement new learner assessments so they can perform their jobs more effectively.

Administrative Preparation—Beyond Tradition. Over the past two decades, the preparation of community college administrators has followed along the lines of K–12 educational leadership training and higher education (university) administrator preparation. Using these programs as models, an emphasis on routine administrative functions has been paramount. Like school principals or university provosts, community college administrators are taught to plan, budget, supervise personnel, direct student services, evaluate programs, and so forth. These functions are important, but practitioners demand that this information be more applicable to the community college environment (Hankin, 1996; Palmer and Katsinas, 1996). For example, they need to know how knowledge about planning, budgeting, and instructional supervision applies to partnerships with external organizations such as schools and businesses. Without abandoning what is most important from the past, professional development providers (from local community colleges to graduate schools) need to pay closer attention to the particulars of community college leadership. Consistent with the notion of leadership for change, an expanded knowledge base on community college administration should be directed squarely at educational change. In the context of preparing leaders as facilitators of change, professional development should focus as much on the interrelationships of critical knowledge areas (such as mission, instruction, and assessment) as on the specific areas themselves. Solutions to problems often come through creative understanding of how change occurs through competing forces and circumstances. For example, deans need to know how organizational policies affect planning and budgeting, which also have an impact on instruction, support services, and student learning. There is nothing new in this observation, yet professional development providers, especially graduate programs, often fail to integrate subject matter in ways that administrators find useful to their everyday work. Curricula are dissected and parceled out into discrete parts, leaving students with the bewildering job of putting the knowledge back together into a meaningful whole. Rarely is the most critical knowledge combined into meaningful interdisciplinary courses or a comprehensive, well-integrated program of study. Community college deans need more than finite bits of knowledge. They need to know how changes in one aspect of the organization have an impact on others. By looking at problems through different lenses, deans can better effect change in valuable ways.

Designing Comprehensive Professional Development Systems

Elements of a comprehensive professional development system for community college deans have existed for some time; what is missing is a concerted effort to link the elements together into a coherent and meaningful whole. Taking my own state of Illinois as an example, several community colleges provide exceptional professional development opportunities for their own personnel. At the state and national levels, state agencies and professional associations provide opportunities for presidents, administrators, and faculty to address concerns of greatest importance to them. Some universities offer graduate programs for community college personnel. As we look to the future, it is important to consider what these different elements of the system contribute already and to consider what new opportunities could emerge if the parts became more coherent.

At the local level, some community colleges offer creative opportunities for their personnel to develop leadership skills, largely as an investment in the future of the institutions. For example, Waubonsee Community College in Illinois offers an annual retreat for administrators (executives, deans, and department chairs) that focuses on leadership development to strengthen the relationships among campus administrators (Kazmerski, 1998). The agenda for the three-day retreat includes information on empowerment, dealing with change, diversity, and communications. Team building is pivotal to achieving the institution's goals, and it is given a top priority at these annual getaways. To reinforce what is learned throughout the year, weekly cabinet meetings include a brief presentation on some aspect of organizational leadership. Monthly meetings provide time for more in-depth discussions about issues of special interest to the group. Waubonsee's president takes an active role in leadership development within the institution. He supports the notion of a comprehensive professional development approach, encouraging personnel to engage in formal graduate study to help them make theory-to-practice linkages that are critical to their work.

Professional development on the local level can be coordinated with efforts of state and national agencies and professional associations. State and national initiatives are particularly helpful to deans, who are often neglected by local professional development programs targeted at faculty and graduate education focused on aspiring executives. The council structure of the American Association of Community Colleges (AACC) provides targeted professional development options, sometimes emphasizing participation by women and minorities (Laden, 1996). The AACC council structure is sometimes replicated within states, where groups of similar personnel interact in various ways (face-to-face meetings, telecommunication networks, the Internet) to pursue common concerns. In Illinois, the development of future community college leaders is the focus of a series of workshops sponsored by the Illinois President's Council and modeled after the Iowa State University's Leadership Institute for New Century (LINC) program. Besides delivering valuable information, state and national professional associations offer opportunities to nurture new leaders, furthering their professional growth.

Finally, graduate education should be integral to a comprehensive professional development system for community college deans. Changes are needed. Recognizing this, in 1997 a group of universities formed the National Conclave on Community College Leadership, with the land grant institutions in Colorado, Illinois, Minnesota, Missouri, Pennsylvania, and Oregon becoming charter members. Either nurturing new or revitalizing existing graduate programs (sometimes called academies), these research universities have benefited from studies conducted by Copa and Ammentorp (1998) on new designs for two-year postsecondary institutions. Combining ideas generated through semiannual meetings, including an annual retreat, faculty from these graduate programs are building curricula based on alternative delivery formats, including weekend and summer sessions, distance learning, and Internet-based instruction. Nearly all of the programs are adopting learning communities consisting of fifteen to twenty-five working professionals who navigate their graduate studies as a cohesive group. For many of the same reasons, learning communities are implemented by community colleges themselves; learning communities flourish in the graduate community college leadership programs at Colorado State University, University of Illinois, University of Minnesota, and Oregon State University. Their success is due largely to their ability to create an intimate, supportive social climate conducive to active learning.

Some graduate programs already encourage students to do internships, but most of the National Conclave programs require them. Building on work-based experiences, project-based learning is pervasive across the courses offered by several of these programs. In fact, learning in alternative formats outside classrooms is encouraged and rewarded. Through the Internet, distance technologies, and work-based learning, these graduate programs are opening up more opportunities for full-time professionals to participate in graduate education and develop in-depth expertise. Consistent with this goal, some doctoral programs of the National Conclave offer alternative residencies. For example, at the University of Illinois at Urbana-Champaign, in lieu of nine months of full-time campus study, doctoral students engage in a year-long special project, focusing on how theory and practice are interrelated. Students conduct projects within their own work setting under the guidance of a local mentor and graduate adviser, and they report their findings in formats that are useful to their employers as well as their graduate schools. Some National Conclave programs such as the Community College Leadership Academy of the University of Minnesota take this idea further, encouraging alternative dissertations emphasizing practical projects based on curriculum development and program evaluation. In so doing, community college personnel are encouraged to focus on issues of greatest concern to them as working professionals. They can nurture a special interest that is directly related to their work and develop expertise that is beneficial to themselves and their institutions.

Conclusion

Deans will play an important role as community colleges continue to evolve. To facilitate their leadership, they need to engage in professional development efforts that focus on the present and future but are informed by the past. A solid commitment to six fundamental knowledge areas is important: mission, philosophy, and history; learner-centered orientation; instructional leadership; educational technologies; accountability and assessment; and administration. Teachings in these areas should be integrated to create a more applicable, interdisciplinary approach. At all levels, a strong commitment should be made to building comprehensive professional development systems. At the local level, community colleges should facilitate focused dialogues on leadership and change. They should also support personnel in pursuing opportunities for further development at the state and national levels. Professional associations should provide special initiatives on topics of particular concern to all of their members, giving women and minorities high priority. Finally, universities should offer graduate programs in formats that cater to the needs of all community college personnel, particularly deans. The goals of graduate education are multifaceted, but any graduate program should be designed to support the endeavors of community college deans to acquire specialized knowledge through learning that links theory and practice. In these ways, deans will be prepared to lead their institutions into the future and better meet the needs of our increasingly diverse nation.

References

Amey, M., and Twombly, S. "Re-visioning Leadership in Community Colleges." *Review of Higher Education,* 1992, *15*(2), 125–150.

Bragg, D., and Colwell, B. "Two-Year Colleges' Initial Experiences with Educational Guarantees." *Community College Journal of Research and Practice,* 1996, *20*(4), 377–395.

Cohen, A., and Brawer, F. *The American Community College.* San Francisco: Jossey-Bass, 1996.

Cohen, A., and others. *Managing Community Colleges: A Handbook for Effective Practice.* San Francisco: Jossey-Bass, 1994.

Copa, G., and Ammentorp, W. (1998). *New Designs for Two-Year Postsecondary Institutions.* Berkeley: National Center for Research in Vocational Education, University of California, Berkeley.

Cross, K. P. *Opening Windows on Learning.* Mission Viejo, Calif.: League for Innovation in the Community College, 1998.

Dougherty, K. "Community College Scenarios: Prospects and Perils Facing a Mature and Complex Institution." Unpublished manuscript. New York: Community College Research Center, Teachers College, Columbia University, 1998.

Gibson-Benninger, B., Ratcliff, J., and Rhoads, R. "Diversity, Discourse, and Democracy: Needed Attributes in the Next Generation of Community College Leadership Programs." In J. Palmer and S. Katsinas (eds.), *Graduate and Continuing Education for Community College Leaders: What It Means Today.* New Directions for Community Colleges, no. 95. San Francisco: Jossey-Bass, 1996.

Green, K. *USC National Survey of Desktop Computing. Teaching, Technology, and Scholarship Project.* Los Angeles: University of Southern California, 1994.

Grubb, W. N. *Honored But Invisible: An Inside Look at Teaching in Community Colleges.* New York: Routledge, 1999.

Grubb, W. N., and others. *Workforce, Economic and Community Development: The Changing Landscape of the Entrepreneurial Community College.* Mission Viejo, Calif.: League for Innovation in the Community College, 1997.

Hankin, J. "The Door That Never Closes: Continuing Education Needs of Community College Leaders." In J. Palme and S. Katsinas (eds.), *Graduate and Continuing Education for Community College Leaders: What It Means Today.* New Directions for Community Colleges, no. 95. San Francisco: Jossey-Bass, 1996.

Harris, S., and Nettles, M. "Ensuring Campus Climates That Embrace Diversity." In L. Rendon and R. Hope (eds.), *Educating a New Majority: Transforming America's Educational System for Diversity.* San Francisco: Jossey-Bass, 1996.

Illinois Task Force on Integration. *Academic and Occupational Integration.* Springfield: Illinois Community College Board, 1997.

Kantor, S. "Rethinking the Role of Instruction for Workforce Training." In T. Zeiss (ed.), *Developing the World's Best Workforce.* Washington, D.C.: American Association of Community Colleges, 1997.

Kazmerski, M. "A Review of Leadership Training Strategies for Administrative Development in Community Colleges." Unpublished manuscript. Champaign: University of Illinois at Urbana-Champaign, 1998.

Laden, B. "The Role of Professional Associations in Developing Academic and Administrative Leaders." In J. Palmer and S. Katsinas (eds.), *Graduate and Continuing Education for Community College Leaders: What It Means Today.* New Directions for Community Colleges, no. 95. San Francisco: Jossey-Bass, 1996.

Layton, J. "The Community College and the Internet." Unpublished doctoral dissertation, University of Illinois at Urbana-Champaign, 1996.

Messick, S. "The Changing Face of Higher Education Assessment." In S. Messick (ed.), *Assessment in Higher Education.* Hillside, N.J.: Erlbaum, 1999.

"9 Issues Affecting Colleges: A Roll Call of the States." *Chronicle of Higher Education,* Aug. 27, 1999, p. 16.

O'Banion, T. *A Learning College for the 21st Century.* Washington, D.C.: American Council on Education, 1997.

Palmer, J., and Katsinas, S. (eds.). *Graduate and Continuing Education for Community College Leaders: What It Means Today.* New Directions for Community Colleges, no. 95. San Francisco: Jossey-Bass, 1996.

Phillippe, K. A. *National Profile of Community Colleges: Trends and Statistics 1997–98.* Washington, D.C.: American Association of Community Colleges, 1997.

Rendon, L., and Garza, H. "Closing the Gap Between Two- and Four-Year Institutions." In L. Rendon and R. Hope (eds.), *Educating a New Majority: Transforming America's Educational System for Diversity.* San Francisco: Jossey-Bass, 1996.

Tinto, V., and Russo, P. "Coordinated Studies Programs: Their Effect on Student Involvement at a Community College." *Community College Review,* 1994, 22(2), 16–25.

DEBRA D. BRAGG is associate professor at the University of Illinois at Urbana-Champaign, where she directs the Office of Community College Research and Leadership.

10

When they are faced with difficult decisions involving conflict, instructional administrators make better-informed and wiser decisions if they can consult a set of basic reference tools.

A Dean's Survival Tool Kit

George L. Findlen

A wise graduate instructor, William Parker Riley, used to say, "If you don't know something, know where to look it up." Administrators cannot know everything. If they did, they would be experts on legal issues as wide ranging as student rights and the Family Educational Rights and Privacy Act, educational access and the Americans with Disabilities Act, management's rights and the Fair Labor Standards Act, and sexual harassment and Title VII of the Civil Rights Act. They would also be experts on topics as wide ranging as the parameters of free speech and academic freedom, as well as what constitutes teaching excellence and how to evaluate it. Not knowing everything, wise administrators need concise resources that provide accurate information for good decisions.

Resources fill our libraries. Tomes range from scholarly treatments, such as Robert M. O'Neil's *Free Speech in the College Community* (Indiana University Press, 1997), to the specific and technical, such as Robert E. Beinstock's *A Guide to Conducting a Hearing in a Higher Education Setting* (College Administration Publications, 1996). When faced with a conflict, administrators need resource material that is brief, understandable, and written for general readers. The resources that follow satisfy these criteria.

Institutional cultures are relatively unique. Thus, not all resources listed here will be useful to all two-year college instructional administrators. The works in this chapter are organized by problem areas that many instructional administrators face today at the turn of the century. Consulting these sources will enable readers to deal effectively with potential conflicts should they arise.

New Directions for Community Colleges, no. 109, Spring 2000 © Jossey-Bass Publishers

Faculty Evaluation

Two-year colleges are teaching institutions, and teaching is the faculty member's primary job responsibility. Thus, all community and technical college instructional administrators should be very knowledgeable of what good teaching is and how it can be assessed. Tenure (renewing appointment) decisions, when unfavorable to the probationary faculty member, are frequently challenged in unionized settings. Instructional administrators who cannot articulate what good teaching is and who are unskilled in discerning it leave themselves open to the charge of being arbitrary and capricious. Of all the knowledge an instructional administrator must master, this is the most important.

An example illustrates the kind of conflict that arises in the process of faculty evaluation. A part-timer no longer used by a division asks to meet with the dean. In the meeting, the person says, "Student ratings of instruction are not valid. I want you to throw away those things you collected in the class I taught a year and a half ago and give me a teaching assignment again. Those students did not appreciate my style and had it in for me. The use of ratings is simply not a valid way of assessing what I do." Can an administrator use student ratings of instruction as part of the reason for not using that instructor again? Do professionally developed student ratings of instruction have validity?

Angelo, T. A., and Cross, K. P. *Classroom Assessment Techniques: A Handbook for College Teachers.* (2nd ed.) San Francisco: Jossey-Bass, 1993.

This book gives faculty a host of mechanisms for getting feedback on the effectiveness of their teaching and of their students' learning. This volume will become increasingly valuable to have when talking to faculty as reflective practice becomes the norm, as accrediting agencies push the importance of assessing student learning, and as faculty get to see themselves as the managers of student learning. The book is especially useful when helping beginning part-timers take control of their teaching.

Baez, B., and Centra, J. A. *Tenure, Promotion, and Reappointment: Legal and Administrative Implications.* ASHE-ERIC Higher Education Report, no. 1. Washington, D.C.: George Washington University, School of Education and Human Development, 1995. (ED 396 608)

This useful volume, which contains basic information for all instructional administrators, has solid sections on the faculty contract of employment, constitutional rights, and employment discrimination. It closes with a section on recommendations for policy and practice.

Cashin, W. "Student Ratings of Teaching: The Research Revisited." IDEA Paper, no. 32. Manhattan, Kans.: Center for Faculty Evaluation and Development, 1995.

Cashin's survey of research conducted from 1988 to 1995 reaffirms his earlier survey of research from 1971 through 1988, also published as an IDEA paper. This publication is among the most up-to-date literature reviews available of empirical research done on student ratings of instruction. Faculty whose teaching evaluations are less than satisfactory frequently challenge the use of student ratings. Empirical research has provided an answer to every challenge, and administrators will benefit by having this research summary close by.

Diamond, R. M. *Serving on Promotion and Tenure Committees: A Faculty Guide*. Bolton, Mass.: Anker Publishing, 1994.

This short book provides a precise statement of what faculty should do when they serve on promotion and tenure committees. One of the best procedural guides available in print, it is an important resource for administrators when dealing with what should be looked at and how. Although written for the university world, it has lessons that administrators in the two-year setting should master. Given the large number of retirements in the late 1990s and beyond, a sloppily done tenure decision will give administrators the next thirty years to regret it.

Hildebrand, M., Wilson, R. C., and Dienst, E. R. *Evaluating University Teaching*. Berkeley: University of California Center for Research and Development in Higher Education, 1971. (ED 057 748)

Just what are the traits of good teaching, and how do we know that? Hildebrand, Wilson, and Dienst's research is perhaps the best study to date identifying traits of effective teaching. Its findings have been reaffirmed in study after study, mostly in journal articles, and its list of behaviors associated with effective teaching remains relevant. The book's brevity recommends it over much later work. Administrators who observe classes and discuss teaching with faculty members should review this little book annually.

McKeachie, W. J. *Teaching Tips: Strategies, Research, and Theory for College and University Teachers*. (9th ed.) Lexington, Mass.: Heath, 1994.

The first edition of this book came out in 1951, and the current edition is still in print, so it has been around continuously for forty-nine years. Although not directly related to instructional evaluation, it is useful when speaking to faculty about teaching to have handy a book about what we know works and what does not. McKeachie sifts through the research and distills it for beginning practitioners.

Sexual Harassment

The rise of accusations, lawsuits, and countersuits for ruined careers means that administrators need to be carefully informed about this volatile issue.

Riggs, R. O., Murrell, P. H., and Cutting, J. C. *Sexual Harassment in Higher Education: From Conflict to Community.* ASHE-ERIC Higher Education Report, no. 2. Washington, D.C.: George Washington University, School of Education and Human Development, 1993. (ED 364 133)

This short work contains a composite model sexual harassment policy and procedure put together from a variety of institutions. Administrators whose institution does not have this sort of book should seriously consider acquiring this one. The chapter on the legal context of sexual harassment is careful and balanced. Administrators trying to decide whether an act constitutes sexual harassment will want to reference this book.

Americans with Disabilities Act (ADA)

The ADA has not always been understood by those responsible for implementing it and by those whom the law was written to protect. Instructional administrators must be prepared to help sort through requests so that the law is honored while at the same time maintaining the integrity of bona-fide educational requirements.

Milt Wright and Associates. *The Americans with Disabilities Act: Making the ADA Work for You.* Northridge, Calif.: Milt Wright and Associates, 1990.

Many tools are available to guide administrators through the requirements of the ADA. This publication focuses on the employer-employee relationship.

Discipline and Termination

Few instructional administrators ever formally discipline a faculty member. Even fewer have to remove faculty for cause. S. Janosic and S. Short's recent article, "Trends in Community College Litigation: Implications for Policy and Practice," *Community College Journal,* 1999, *69,* 26–30, reports that a majority of court cases involving community college faculty deal with issues of discipline and dismissal. If either situation presents itself, the following resources will more than pay for themselves.

Andrews, H. A. *Teachers Can Be Fired! The Quest for Quality.* Chicago: Catfeet Press, 1995.

Although Andrews mixes the literature of K–12 education with that of community college education, he has read the literature for higher education practitioners. His opening chapter, "Getting There from Here: Good and Bad Evaluation Methods," clearly tells those of us who supervise that if there is a problem with evaluation systems, it lies in the laps of supervisors who do not give it the attention it requires. Subsequent chapters emphasize the positive; see Chapter Ten, "Progressive Remediation as Formative Evaluation," for instance. Later chapters deal with termination. His perspective throughout is that of the instructional developer.

Beckham, J. C. *Faculty/Staff Nonrenewal and Dismissal for Cause in Institutions of Higher Education*. Asheville, N.C.: College Administration Publications, 1986.

This book, written entirely from the perspective of the court, is the most concise and useful presentation on the legal bases for removing faculty for cause and the tests that courts will use when dismissed faculty challenge administrative decisions. An administrator faced with removing a tenured faculty member for cause will appreciate this book.

Deblieux, M. *Documenting Discipline*. West Des Moines, Iowa: American Media, 1995.

Although written for business and industrial settings, this is a clear monograph on what steps to follow when faced with having to discipline someone. The author gives examples of his recommended training, counseling, oral warning, written warning, last-step option, and termination sequence for progressive discipline. Administrators in a unionized environment will find this book helpful.

Copyright

The 1989 decision against Kinko's should be a warning to administrators who do not exercise oversight of copying done by faculty and staff in their units.

Hoon, P. (ed). *Guidelines for Educational Use of Copyrighted Materials: Designed for Educators and Librarians in the Higher Education Setting*. Pullman: Washington State University Press, 1997.

This thirty-four-page reference guide by Washington State University's attorney (and copyright expert) covers audiovisual material, music, software, and distance learning, as well as print material. Boxes in the text contain answers to frequently asked questions. The sample letters asking for permission to use material in the classroom are handy. An appendix includes key sections of the Copyright Act. Administrators should consult this work when considering photocopying materials.

Questions and Answers on Copyright for the Campus Community. Washington, D.C.: Association of American Publishers, Oberlin, Ohio: National Association of College Stores, and Software Publisher's Association, 1997.

This edition includes material on software and Internet issues. No administrator should be without this twenty-page collection of lucid questions and answers. Its cost is low enough to justify providing all faculty and staff with a copy.

Student Privacy

Administrators in two-year colleges sometimes get a call from a parent who has paid a child's tuition and wants to know if that son or daughter is attending class regularly. The call may come from an employer who asks what grades an employee received on class work. That is when an administrator should turn to the Family Educational Rights and Privacy Act (FERPA).

Lowery, J. "Implementing FERPA on Campus." *Synthesis: Law and Policy in Higher Education,* 1998, *10.*

This issue of *Synthesis* includes Lowery's outline of what the law requires, an insightful interview with the director of the Family Policy Compliance Office in the U.S. Department of Education, and an excellent summary of the results of legal challenges brought under FERPA. It is one of the clearest, most useful brief guides to FERPA.

Student Discipline

Increasingly, smaller two-year colleges merge the chief of academic affairs and the student affairs administrator into one position. Situations such as the following scenario make the next item useful for most academic managers. A faculty member withdrew a student from his class for excessive absences in accordance with his written policy. The following day, the student interrupted a lab while in session and screamed obscenities at the instructor, threatening a lawsuit if the instructor did not reverse himself. On hearing of the matter, the dean of academic and student affairs wants to discipline the student. What are the student's minimum due process rights that the dean must observe in order not to be overturned by a court? How should the dean proceed?

Amanda, G. *Coping with the Disruptive College Student: A Practical Model.* Asheville, N.C.: College Administration Publications, 1994.

From time to time, instructional administrators need to remove students from classes. This book explains five principles of student conduct, has a clear chapter on procedures that should be followed when a student is disruptive, and explains what is required (and what is not) for due process. Administrators need only one major case of a disruptive student to make them want to turn to a book like this one.

General Legal Resources

Most administrators are faced sooner or later with someone who says, "That's against the law. You can't do that." Many instructional supervisors are from small institutions and do not have immediate access to legal counsel with expertise in higher education law. The following works provide an overview for general readers.

Bickel, R. D., Young, D. P., and Gehring, D. D. *The College Administrator and the Courts: Basic Casebook* and *The College Administrator and the Courts: Briefs of Selected Court Cases Affecting the Administration of Institutions of Higher Education.* Asheville, N.C.: College Administration Publications, 1988–.

The first volume of this two-volume set is a synthesis and overview of court cases on issues that have come up in institutions of higher education-collective bargaining and employment discrimination, for example. The volume ends in a lengthy set of appendices reprinting laws that have been used in legal decisions. The second volume contains the four issues of briefs issued each year since 1988. Each brief of a case contains the facts, the core issue to be decided, the court's response and reasoning. Briefs are typically one-page in length. Instructional administrators threatened with legal action will want access to this two-volume set.

Bureau of National Affairs (BNA) Editorial Staff. *Grievance Guide.* (9th ed.) Washington, D.C.: Bureau of National Affairs, 1995.

This volume, updated regularly since it first came out in 1959, is a distillation of arbitration decisions. Not surprisingly, the longest section deals with discipline and dismissal, but there are sections on promotions, seniority, and management rights (among others) as well. Each section contains an "In Brief" outline of arbitration results and detailed examples taken from actual arbitrations. When union grievance representatives threaten to "go to arbitration," instructional administrators should turn to this useful volume.

Kaplin, W. A., and Lee, B. A. *The Law of Higher Education: A Comprehensive Guide to Legal Implications of Administrative Decision Making.* (3rd ed.) San Francisco: Jossey-Bass, 1995.

Designed as a comprehensive textbook on postsecondary law, Kaplin and Lee's book has been the standard since 1978. Every chapter ends with a selected annotated bibliography. Readers should consider this heavy tome a starting point for understanding a problem area. The authors correctly caution readers that the law continues to evolve such that their thorough treatment is not the final word. No college library or instructional administrative team should be without a copy of this basic book.

Weeks, K. M. *Managing Departments: Chairpersons and the Law.* Nashville, Tenn.: College Legal Information, 1997.

A cross between the Kaplin-Lee book and the Bickel case briefs, this book contains a two- or three-page statement on what the law requires on each of fourteen topics that most division and department chairs will face, and follows the statement with a one- or two-page summary of a key court case. Front-line administrators may find this volume more useful than the Kaplin-Lee book or Bickel case briefs.

GEORGE L. FINDLEN is the dean of general education and educational services at Western Wisconsin Technical College. He and his colleague, Rose Ann Findlen, a vice president of student services at Madison Area Technical College, consult with two-year colleges, leading case study workshops on problems that instructional administrators face.

INDEX

Back Issue/Subscription Order Form

Copy or detach and send to:
Jossey-Bass Inc., Publishers, 350 Sansome Street, San Francisco CA 94104-1342

Call or fax toll free!
Phone 888-378-2537 6AM-5PM PST; Fax 800-605-2665

Back issues: Please send me the following issues at $25 each
(Important: please include series initials and issue number, such as CC90)

1. CC _____

_____

_____

$ _____ Total for single issues

$ _____ Shipping charges (for single issues *only;* subscriptions are exempt
from shipping charges): Up to $30, add $5^{50} • $30^{01}–$50, add $6^{50}
$50^{01}–$75, add $7^{50} • $75^{01}–$100, add $9 • $100^{01}–$150, add $10
Over $150, call for shipping charge

Subscriptions   Please ❑ start   ❑ renew my subscription to *New Directions
for Community Colleges* for the year ___ at the following rate:

❑ Individual $60   ❑ Institutional $107

NOTE: Subscriptions are quarterly, and are for the calendar year only.
Subscriptions begin with the spring issue of the year indicated above.
For shipping outside the U.S., please add $25.

$ _____ Total single issues and subscriptions (CA, IN, NJ, NY and DC
residents, add sales tax for single issues. NY and DC residents must
include shipping charges when calculating sales tax. NY and Canadian
residents only, add sales tax for subscriptions)

❑ Payment enclosed (U.S. check or money order only)

❑ VISA, MC, AmEx, Discover Card #_____ Exp. date_____

Signature _____ Day phone _____

❑ Bill me (U.S. institutional orders only. Purchase order required)

Purchase order #_____

Name _____

Address _____

_____

Phone_____ E-mail _____

For more information about Jossey-Bass Publishers, visit our Web site at:
www.josseybass.com   **PRIORITY CODE = ND1**